LEADING SCHOOLS IN THE

THE WORK OF THE BURSAR: A JACK OF ALL TRADES?

ESSAYS IN LEADERSHIP FOR CHANGING TIMES

Edited by
Jonathan Cook and Nigel Richardson
with members of the
Independent Schools' Bursars Association

Published for the Independent Schools' Bursars Association
and the Headmasters' and Headmistresses' Conference
by John Catt Educational Ltd

2011

First Published 2011

by John Catt Educational Ltd,
12 Deben Mill Business Centre, Old Maltings Approach,
Melton, Woodbridge, Suffolk IP12 1BL
Tel: 01394 389850 Fax: 01394 386893
Email: enquiries@johncatt.com
Website: www.johncatt.com

Reprinted 2015

ISBN: 978 1 908095 15 2
eISBN: 978 1 908095 16 9

Set and designed by
John Catt Educational Limited

Printed and bound in Great Britain
by Ashford Colour Press

CONTENTS

About the Contributors

Roy Blackwell is clerk to the United Westminster Schools/Grey Coat Hospital Foundation, and also to each of its school's governing bodies. The Foundation is unusual in that it contains independent and maintained schools and because the maintained schools are inner London comprehensives. He started his working life as a teacher, after which he became education officer for a local authority before spending ten years in the civil service, which led to him travelling around Europe, negotiating bi-lateral and multi-lateral treaties for HM Government.

Jonathan Cook was the general secretary of ISBA from 2005-2010. Prior to this, he was a soldier for 34 years and then the bursar at a wide age-range day/boarding school. He holds a Master's degree in human resource management; is a fellow of two chartered institutes; a company secretary; a governor of his local Church of England infant school and a trustee of the Ramblers Holidays Charitable Trust.

Bruno Delacave is the bursar of Norwich School. He worked for Ernst & Young for 12 years, first qualifying as a chartered accountant in London, then as a member of their corporate advisory and mergers and acquisitions practices in London, Geneva and New York. He left to be CFO of an investment company in Geneva, before moving to London in 1999 as CFO of an interactive TV company owned by Sky, BT, Panasonic and HSBC. He was then appointed finance director of an AIM listed venture capital company before becoming the bursar of Gresham's School. In September 2005 he was appointed bursar and development officer of Norwich School. He is a member of the CFDG (Charity Finance Directors' Group) and was elected to the ISBA executive committee in 2009.

Andy Dorgan is the business director of Bristol Cathedral Choir School. He is a graduate in sociology from the University of York and was a CIPFA trainee with Coventry City Council, qualifying in 1996. Previously the bursar at Woodway Park School, Coventry and Frome

Community College, he took up his current appointment in 2008, just after the school had become a state academy.

David Goucher was bursar of Bryanston from 1987 to 1996. After school education at Netherthorpe Grammar School, Chesterfield, he graduated from the RAF College, Cranwell, in 1958. After a series of other postings, he worked at the RAF Staff College, Bracknell, and the Joint Services Staff College, Latimer, leaving the services as a group captain and having been commanding officer, RAF Uxbridge, from 1982-3. He was a member of the ISBA committee in 1995-6 and a regular contributor to *Conference & Common Room* in the 1990s.

Annika Hedrich-Wiggans studied music at Cambridge and Oxford Universities before joining PricewaterhouseCoopers, where she qualified as a chartered accountant in 2000. She went on to work as finance bursar at University College School, Hampstead; was bursar of Kelly College, Tavistock, from 2004-9, and then became bursar of Oakham School. She has a strong interest in the continuing growth of staff training and professional development opportunities for all support staff in independent schools. She has served on the ISBA executive committee since 2007; chairs its finance sub-committee and represents the ISBA on the Boarding Schools' Association board of directors.

Wing Commander Bryan Login MA MBA FCIS MBIFM (RAF Ret'd) is the bursar and clerk to the governors, Truro High School (400+ girls: 3-18). Following a long, but thoroughly enjoyable, career in the Royal Air Force, which included tours of duty in the Falklands, Germany, Cyprus, Saudi Arabia, Holland and Iraq, he retired early to takeup a 'proper job'. Having served at RAF St Mawgan, the call of the south-west was too much to resist, so when his current post in Cornwall became available, the rest, as they say, is history.

Ray Maher is bursar and clerk to the governors at King Edward VI School, Southampton. Following a degree at Manchester University he went on to qualify as a chartered accountant with Coopers & Lybrand Deloitte. In 1992 he became bursar of Liverpool Anglican Cathedral, involved in establishing a number of charitable and commercial companies to partner housing, health and education in the city. He was a governor of a local CofE primary school and joined Nord Anglia Education Plc before becoming commercial director of Howell's School in Denbigh. At King Edward's he is also chair of Youth and Families Matter Ltd, a charitable company incorporated in 2008, working closely with local schools and families. He is passionate about the power of education to transform lives.

Alison Martin is chairman of ISBA in 2010-2011, having previously been vice chairman in 2009-10; chairman of the finance committee in 2008-9, and chairman of the GP committee in 2007-8. Educated at Battle Abbey and Bromley High School, followed by the London College of Secretaries, she initially worked for NatWest bank as a secretary before having three children now in their late 20s and early 30s. Then during 14 years as a housewife, fundraiser, organiser, family taxi driver and general dogsbody she studied and qualified as an accounting technician. She gained an MBA in education management and, in 1999, was appointed as bursar at St Mary's Calne and its associated preparatory school, St Margaret's. She moved to Warminster School in October 2007.

Richard Mayfield has been the head of operations at Abbotsholme School in Staffordshire for the past two years. Previously he has worked for British Sugar, Selfridges and Nottingham Rehabilitation Supplies. A qualified management accountant, he has a degree in economics from Loughborough University. He is married to his wife of nine years, Jo, and has three young children. He enjoys spending time with friends and family, snowboarding (when the opportunity arises), listening to a wide variety of music and supporting Birmingham City Football Club.

Richard Metcalfe has been bursar and clerk to the governors at Newcastle upon Tyne Royal Grammar School since 1999, during which time the school has undergone an extensive programme of refurbishment and development. Prior to his present post he spent 28 years in the estates and buildings department at Durham University, the last ten as its director. He was closely involved in staff development in the HE sector (in particular for estates staff), and has served as a governor of two schools and two colleges. He is a fellow of the British Institute of Facilities Management and currently secretary to the north-east region of ISBA.

Paul Motte has been director of college operations at UWC Atlantic College since May 2008. Before that he was bursar at Carmel College, Wallingford, and at Leighton Park School, Reading. He completed an MBA in education management at the University of Lincoln in 2004, and is a member of the Chartered Management Institute and a fellow of the Institute of Administrative Management. He was elected to ISBA's executive committee in May 2001; chaired the general purposes sub-committee in 2003/4; was vice-chairman of the Association in 2004/5, and chairman the following year.

John Pratten has been bursar and clerk to the governors at Box Hill School since June 1997 having previously spent two years as the operations director of a field marketing company (*ie* the practical side of sales promotion rather than anything to do with agriculture!) and three years as a purveyor of the Black Arts (Public Relations). He retired from the Regular Army in 1988 and from the TA in 2010.

Nigel Richardson was chairman of HMC in 2007 and has been co-editor of all the books in this series. He was Head of the Perse School, Cambridge, from 1994 until 2008, after posts at Uppingham, Dragon School, Oxford, and The King's School in Macclesfield. An appraiser of Heads and teachers, a governor of several HMC schools and a syndic of the Cambridge University Press, he edited the HMC magazine *Conference & Common Room* from 1999-2002. He has written history books for children and training literature for the Industrial Society, and is working on a biography of the great Victorian Headmaster, Edward Thring.

Alison Shakespeare is the business director at Leicester Grammar School, an independent coeducational day school for pupils aged 3-18. She read geography at Fitzwilliam College, Cambridge, before training as a chartered accountant with Coopers & Lybrand (now part of PricewaterhouseCoopers). She has worked as a forensic accountant and in senior finance roles at the Arts Council and *Connexions*. When she joined LGS as business director in April 2006, the school was in the early stages of a project to relocate. LGS moved to a new, purpose-built, site in September 2008, since when pupil numbers have risen by 20%.

Mark Taylor has been bursar at the King's School, Canterbury, since 2010. He started his professional life as a re-insurance broker in London before joining the Army for eight years in 1984. His career in bursaring includes being deputy bursar at Cranbrook School (1993); bursar at Dulwich Prep School, Cranbrook, (1996); and bursar and clerk to the governors at Bedales Schools (2003), where he had responsibility for the pre-prep, prep and senior schools. In September 2005 he delivered a RIBA award-winning administration and classroom building at a cost that was less per square metre than the DCSF benchmark. He was elected as a fellow of the Royal Society for the encouragement of the Arts, Manufacturing and Commerce (FRSA) in October 2008. He has been a member of the ISBA's executive committee since 2007.

Yvonne Thomas has been bursar at Wrekin College since 2004, having previously worked as chief accountant for the Allied Schools Group for six years. She qualified as a chartered accountant in 1980 and gained audit experience with KPMG in Birmingham. She then moved into industry and worked as financial controller and subsequently director in the steel and mining equipment sectors. A company sponsorship enabled her to complete an MBA with Aston University in 1995. Since 2008 she has served as a trustee and treasurer of the Ironbridge Gorge Museum, one of the largest independent museums in the world.

Mike Vacher left the Army in 2005 to become the bursar of the King's School, Ely. During the latter years of his military service he was the chief of staff (effectively the bursar) at the Royal Military Academy, Sandhurst, and was seconded to Jordan to act as project officer for the establishment of a leadership academy on comparable lines – albeit heeding the culture of the region! He is now the bursar of the Prior Park Educational Trust in Bath.

Introduction

Nigel Richardson

This is the seventh volume in the *Leading Schools* series, following on from previous titles that focused on Heads; Senior Management Teams; Heads of Department; Newly Qualified Teachers; those involved in Pastoral Work and, most recently, those in Public Relations, Marketing and Development. The involvement of John Catt Educational Ltd as publisher, and of the Headmasters' and Headmistresses' Conference (HMC) as co-sponsor, have been a continuing feature of the series.

This book is co-sponsored by the Independent Schools' Bursars Association (until 1983, the Public Schools' Bursars' Association), which was founded in 1932 at a meeting at Epsom College. It came into being to support the growing number of schools in which the Head had once controlled the financial as well as the educational management, but which had, over the previous few decades, created the post of bursar.

The ISBA now has over 900 members, including some 30 overseas associate members. Moreover, because some institutions have more than one 'school' registered with the DfE, the ISBA looks after rather more than 1000 of the 1265 Independent Schools Council (ISC) schools and is one of its constituent members.

It is a charitable company limited by guarantee, whose objects are the advancement of education by the promotion of efficient and effective financial management, administration and ancillary services in independent schools. It is schools, rather than individuals, that are members of the ISBA, although their usual point of contact with the Association is the bursar. Chapter 17 describes the range of benefits and advice that ISBA can offer.

Since then, as the next section will show, the range and demands of the bursar's job have grown out of all recognition. In larger schools there is now a team of people rather than one individual responding to them; in many, the person at the top of the pyramid is known by a different title. In some schools, a group of individuals in specialist support roles are collectively and individually answerable to the Head as chief executive.

Wondering whether we could or should reflect these developments, we considered the title of this book carefully. Ultimately, however, having recently surveyed its members, ISBA's view was that the term 'Bursar' is still the most widely used and widely understood. We hope that the term will be seen as generic both to the person(s) and to the roles described.

We hope, too that the book's sub-title *Jack of all trades?* causes no raised eyebrows. In terms of gender, yes: these days there are many Jills, as well as Jacks, occupying in the bursar's chair. Furthermore if, when one hears the phrase, one often thinks of the words which tend immediately to follow it: 'Master of none', it is worth remembering the saying in fullest version: 'Jack of all trades, Master of none; though oftentimes better than master of one'. Bursars truly are practitioners of many parts.

As with previous books in this series, we have encouraged writers to centre their advice on their own experience: to write as they feel. Their work has been edited with a fairly light touch – more with house style in mind – than in an attempt to eliminate all areas of overlap. It will not take sizeable powers of observation to detect some significant themes that recur, sometimes from more than two writers.

Jonathan Cook, to whom I owe a great debt for all his support for this book during his final weeks as the ISBA general secretary, touches on the significance of this in his concluding section, but meanwhile we make no apology for it: the fact that a number of writers wish to venture into similar territory has a value in signifying the most pressing pre-occupations, dilemmas and balances with which many of today's bursars have to deal. More discerning readers may also spot interesting differences of emphasis along the way.

I am also very grateful to Gerald Ellison, bursar of The Perse School, Cambridge, who advised me in the final stages of putting this book together on some of the technical complexities of the role that I managed to avoid having to grasp as a Head, but cannot evade as an editor.

We hope that the chapters that follow will inform, challenge, sometimes cause you to disagree and above all make you think – and that you will enjoy them, as well as benefiting from them.

As you do so, two things go almost without saying in these challenging economic times, but I shall write them nevertheless. First, that the work of our bursars has never been more important; second, that we should never lose sight of the fact that whilst it may take many decades to build up the plant, personnel and reputation of a great school, if its finances, fabric and legal responsibilities are neglected, it may well take only a very short time to close it down.

Chapter 1

An overview: Bursars and Heads

Nigel Richardson

Many stories have grown up over the years about C C 'Skipper' Lynam, Headmaster of the famous Dragon School, Oxford, from 1887 until 1921, and his novel management of finance. It is claimed that, when faced with difficulties over paying salaries, he solved the problem by the simple expedient of borrowing off one master to pay another. That as he made his way north to join his beloved yacht *The Blue Dragon* in Scotland each year, he made out the boys' bills with no data other than the guess inside his head about the wealth or poverty of each parent. Even that when he once accidentally dropped the entire batch of end-of-term reports and bills into the waters of Oban harbour, he merely wrote to every parent saying, 'Your boy is doing splendidly. Please pay me what you think you owe'.

Over 100 years later, it is hard to separate truth from legend – but as the school's historian observes, no legend has ever been born out of a vacuum. One thing is more certain: the Skipper operated in a far more carefree and unregulated age than our own. Even so, after a few years in the post, he finally accepted the need to copy what many other Heads were doing at the start of the 20th century. He appointed a bursar.

Different challenges over many decades

Plenty has been written about the variety of challenges that Heads faced at various times during the 20th century: in rallying their staff and pupils in the face of the huge former-pupil casualties in the Great War; when confronted by the bewildering array and extent of demands to modernise their schools during the turbulent social change of the 1960s; or in recent times through the demands of league tables and inspection.

Far less, however, has been recorded about the work of the bursars during that period – partly because it is often said that the best bursars are the ones who cover all the ground and keep their Heads on track, whilst selflessly keeping the lowest of profiles themselves. Yet the challenges that bursars have faced are no less remarkable.

At the end of the Victorian era, they had to respond to the growing public expectations about standards of public health, at a time when many schools were still regularly prone to epidemics. The 1902 Education Act brought greatly increased competition in the shape of the large number of direct grant and new grammar schools.

In the Great War, they had to find money to support the children of bereaved mothers, and to deal patiently with fathers who had fallen on hard times. Sir George Sitwell wrote to Eton in 1915 that, because he had been hit financially so hard by the conflict, he intended henceforth to pay fees for his son in pigs and potatoes, rather than cash. At the same time bursars were frantically trying to make up for staff gone-absent or returned-wounded; to cope with rationing; to turn games fields over to vegetable growing.

In the 1920s, there was a brief boom in demand for independent school places. However, having masterminded the construction of expensive war memorials, bursars helped to settle battle-scarred veterans back into school communities and struggled to return everything to normal at a time when the number of state school bursaries had rapidly increased.

Then they faced the Depression of the 1930s: a new generation of parents (an earlier version of today's 'squeezed middle class') came knocking, with tales of woe about unemployment, high death duties and falling profits from farming. Rolls began to fall – to the extent that in the late 1930s HMC even contemplated asking the national government for a Royal Commission to look at possible government subsidies, or setting up an impartial, independent body to arbitrate in recruitment disputes between schools: maybe even to decide centrally which schools should downsize.

The 1939-45 war again brought rationing and disappearing staff. Some schools were requisitioned by the military; others left their familiar urban surroundings to share buildings with rural boarding schools that had quite different traditions from their own. There was widespread bomb damage and plenty more Digging for Victory. Then, as soon as peace returned, came the terrible winter of 1947.

Over the decades that followed, schools embarked on what some see as a headlong flight into a competition to see who could build biggest and most lavishly: theatres and sports centres proliferated. Governors sometimes looked to bursars to perform miracles in financing and project-managing these new ventures in the face of high inflation and rapidly rising building prices – and then, of course, to cope with their hefty running costs.

Simultaneously, parents became far less passive consumers and started to demand markedly better boarding facilities. Pupils no longer automatically went to the school that their parents had attended, and they began to look around again for pastures-new at the age of 16. To respond to these trends, and in recognition of other ways in which the world was changing, ambitious Heads called for study bedrooms, expensive new science labs, and later on (albeit for the most positive of reasons) the ICT budget began to run away with itself.

Recognising that fee rises could not be infinite, schools began to set up development or appeal offices, or on-going foundations to fund capital development in whole or in part; these brought with them a whole new range of initiatives – and additional specialist staff whom it generally fell to the bursar to line-manage.

From the 1970s onwards, salaries and employers' pension contributions rose faster and became harder to predict – most notoriously during the Heath government of 1970-4 when, at a time of very high inflation, a teacher's pay cheque could change every month in response to the latest rise in the retail price index. A brief reminiscence may give an idea of how much has changed since then, both in terms of salary arrangements and as a result of inflation.

I went into teaching in 1971 (annual salary: £1250), in a school in which all assistant staff were paid £200 at the start of term, followed at the end of week nine by the termly balance owed to them. Someone's bright idea that everyone might henceforth be paid monthly was greeted by a response from some senior members of the common room that such a vulgar arrangement was not appropriate for gentlemen. A counterproposal emerged that the £200 start-of-term payment be raised to £300 – at which point we junior staff pointed out that this would actually mean us paying money *back* to the school in week nine. After that, the school soon joined the rest of the human race, in terms of having a monthly payroll.

The volume of regulation has been transformed since those days, too. Schools have been deluged with demands for more rigorous compliance; a huge range of written policies, and the challenge of managing health and safety and risk assessment. Since the Children Act 1989, child protection procedures have added very substantial time and cost demands, which successive governments have ramped up in response to a series of high-profile and tragic incidents (see chapter 4).

There has been a huge new raft of employment legislation (chapter 11), demanding increasingly specialist skills. Parents have gained greatly increased rights: to complain formally if something annoys them or if they perceive that a school has served them poorly; to appeal after a pupil is required to leave a school. Whether or not the bursar is also clerk to the governing body, such cases can demand a very large amount of his/her time.

The growth of the organisation – and the changing nature of bursars

The scale and nature of these demands varies from school to school, and not every school has faced them all at once. Some of the challenges already identified affected the Head just as much as the bursar – although not always in the same way. In many schools, the changes have been accompanied by burgeoning senior management teams and increased governor support.

Within the bursary itself, bursars have not had to face these challenges alone; in larger institutions they have acquired either a finance bursar or an estates manager, or a human resources officer – or a combination of all three – who line-manage those responsible for catering, grounds, the medical centre, caretakers and cleaners, and much more.

In many cases it is on these people that much of the detailed new work has devolved. However, all these new middle-management posts need their holder being line-managed too, and their holders being appraised. The buck has grown bigger, and ultimately, all of it tends to stop with the bursar, who remains in charge of all the non-teaching/support arms of the school.

Time was when the great majority of bursars – in the larger and most-established schools, at least – came from a military background. The best of them proved to be adept at handling this very dramatic change in their lives, and reinvented themselves as gifted generalists. One of my early tasks as a Head was to attempt the long-listing for the replacement of the very long-standing bursar who had stayed on for an extra year to see me in.

As the armed services began to downsize in the late 1980s, there was no shortage of applicants and, as someone whose own military background was limited to three years in a school CCF, I struggled to choose between swathes of different military experience: men who appeared to have held conventional military commands; men who had done undercover work in Northern Ireland; one who had organised dog patrols in the Far East; another who had commanded an artillery school on Rainham Marshes.

From memory, over two decades later, in a field of nearly 200 all of them were *men*. Since then, things have markedly changed: right across the sector, a succession of people of both genders, with financial and other skills and backgrounds, have brought exciting new dimensions to the bursar's role. One thing has *not* changed, however. Even with an increased number of people to whom to delegate, it is in the nature of good bursars to be prepared to get their hands dirty when the common purpose or a sudden emergency demands it.

I once interviewed a candidate (he happened to be from a very senior military background) for a bursar's post in a small and far from well-resourced school in which the bursary consisted of three people. His response to every "What would you do, if...?" question was the same: "I'd get a man to do it." He would surely have been a square peg in a round hole – and if the round hole had been a blocked drain, it somehow seems unlikely that his would have been the sleeves rolled up, not that his arm would have been pushed down it to sort the problem out.

Never take your bursar for granted

As a very experienced ISBA member observed on an INSET course for new Heads that I once attended, it is the bursars who often pick up the jobs that Heads have no time, experience, expertise or interest to take on. He asked very persuasively (and I have to paraphrase many years later): "I can only urge you Heads occasionally to remind yourselves that bursars both need and deserve your support. The person on whom you are tempted to dump anything that you regard as too trivial for your attention may well have come from a very senior post in another walk of life. Earlier in his or her career, s/he may well have handled responsibility and controlled a budget at a level which you may never come near to experiencing."

I tried to remember that, and every September at the start of term staff meeting, to remind everyone of what had been achieved over the holidays while many of us had been sunning ourselves on beaches around the world. I redoubled my efforts after a summer that had involved the bursar and estates manager in a multi-million pound building project with minimal holidays themselves, when I heard a deeply-tanned member of staff complaining on the day before term began about a window catch still not fixed...

Stereotypes and humorists

It is all too easy to create stereotypes around the roles of Head and bursar: the one visionary but impractical in financial terms, and the other one rather too practical and not visionary enough. All stereotypes have their exceptions, too – such as the Head who used to spend the first afternoon of every HMC conference finalising his farm accounts, or the bursar who might well have won BBC TV's *Mastermind* with his vast knowledge of the novels of Anthony Trollope.

At this point, however, let us allow ourselves a brief diversion into the realm of stereotypical humour, but ultimately (as you will see) for a serious purpose.

Over the years, bursars have frequently been the object of black humour – the equivalent of the goalkeeper in professional football – and not only from the writer who claimed that, 'Bursars fall into three categories: fiddly-diddly, drinky-winky and naughty-naughty'.

They can be portrayed as bleak and unyielding. Remember the Head, writing in 2006 in *Conference & Common Room* about his journey to the HMC conference in rainy Manchester: 'I took the train north from Birmingham and entered the bronchial zone of dark grey northern skies the colour of a bursar's soul.' Or rapacious: as in the parent who replied to a request for the payment of late fees: 'I think the fees are extortionate, but I shall continue to pay as I have done in the past – through the nose.'

The necessity for, and ability of, a good bursar sometimes to say "no" can attract cynicism, as in the notice from a wit on a common room board, over the bursar's signature: 'Owing to the current financial stringencies, the light at the end of the tunnel will be switched off until further notice.'

A few are perceived to be inflexible and oblivious to the consequences of their decisions – as in another spoof notice: 'Would staff and pupils please note that due to the severe financial cutbacks, only the centre octave of the piano will be tuned during the coming term. Pianists using both hands are advised to use the outer extremities of the instrument, since the centre section may be required for concerts.'

You can also see some bursars as having one-track minds, as in the conversation in which the Head says:

"Bursar, we've decided that we're going to have the IB."

And the bursar replies:

"That's fine, just so long as it's diesel and can mow the first XI square."

Bursars, being resourceful, and skilled at improvisation, are quite able to look after themselves, though. Some years ago, the ISBA magazine published a glossary of terms and definitions sent in by bursars:

- The words '*slightly overstated*': term used by the Headmaster to excuse his earlier wildly optimistic forecast of pupil numbers.
- *Understated*: term used by the bursar to describe a budget for which he is responsible to the governors but which others have hugely and wantonly overspent.
- *Head's amenity fund*: the budget to which everything that the Head wants, but has forgotten to budget for, goes. Usually understated.
- *Action Points*: summary of a meeting taken by someone other than the bursar who can't be bothered to write proper minutes.
- *All rounder scholarships*: awards for pupils who aren't good at anything in particular.

- *Beauty parade*: a succession of unattractive accountants, solicitors or caterers who pitch up on a given day to convince you that they are much better than the shower you have at the moment. Much loved by governors.
- *ICT*: an essential symbol of a school's virility for the Head to show off to parents: a bottomless pit.
- *Risk assessment*: a task carried out with unfailing reluctance by teachers who think that the bursar alone is responsible for safety.

The bursars' assessments of the people around them?

- *Staff lunch*: a daily contest to see how much a teacher can get on his plate.
- *GAP students*: indispensable post-pubescent non-English speakers who work long unsocial hours for no pay, and leave owing a large phone bill.
- *Biscuits*: essential indicator of the importance of your meeting: chocolate – governors; jammy dodgers – visiting fellow-bursars; plain digestives – bursary staff; none – teachers.
- *Auditors*: a team of pre-pubescents who turn up every October to try and fathom out what you have been doing for the past 12 months.
- *Bursar's secretary*: the pitbull who guards your door against intruding teachers and other unwelcome visitors.
- *Bursar and clerk to the governors*: the poor sucker who has to be able to write, speak, eat and drink, all at the same time during governors' working lunches.

To be fair, the magazine also included:

- *Out*: code in the bursar's diary to indicate that he is not in school, but does not want anyone to know that he has gone down to the driving range and will be popping into Sainsbury's on the way back – and, no, he probably won't be back in time to see the head of biology about his drain problem.
- *Health and Safety meeting*: code in the bursar's diary to describe his monthly golf day. Not to be confused with a Health and Safety Meeting (upper case): a tiresome termly event at which all the action points from the previous meeting get carried over to the next.

You get the drift – and you will get more of it in the afterword to this book, where a former bursar gives a spectacularly sideways view of the constituencies with which he and his colleagues deal day-by-day.

A common purpose

The serious point that comes out of all this two-way humour is this: in those schools that function most effectively, the Head and the rest of SMT – including the bursar – have complementary skills. They have a good sense of what is properly their own territory and what is not. They enjoy a mutual respect; they thrive on different challenges and they are even prone to worry about different things.

There is a sense of common purpose: the Head may dream dreams, and the bursar may sometimes have to keep the dreamer's feet firmly on the ground, but they have a sense of common purpose, and the bursar instinctively tries to provide the means to achieve the dream rather than merely to thwart it. Some of the great Victorian Heads, (notably Thring of Uppingham) might have achieved even more, and caused themselves and their families far less financial anxiety over what they *did* achieve, if they had been prepared to work with someone who possessed the all-round skills of the best of today's bursars.

By contrast, where bursar and Head profoundly dislike each other; where they operate out of physically distant baronial empires at opposite ends of the school; where the bursar fundamentally looks down on the teaching workforce or *vice versa* (I think of the otherwise excellent bursar who, in an unguarded moment of stress many years ago, described schoolteachers as "b----- peasants"), life tends to be far less smooth.

On one thing the Heads', governors' and bursars' professional associations are all agreed: ultimately, there can only be one person in charge of the organisation on a day-to-day basis. The wise bursar knows that that person is the Head – or chief executive, or whatever title the Head has – and that the Head is responsible to the governors.

But the wise Head also recognises that it has to be a team operation; that the bursar carries a huge workload, unpredictable pressures and very big responsibilities, and that *in extremis* if the Head seems to be acting in a way that will imperil the school financially, reputationally or in some other way, the bursar *may* have to consider alerting the chairman of the governors. This in turn reflects the fact that in a school that is truly progressing, the chairman, Head and bursar constitute a virtuous triangle of roles.

Whilst compiling this chapter, I asked Jonathan Cook whether any history of the ISBA was currently in existence. He answered in the negative – but also pointed me towards the definition of the Cellarer in *The Rule of Saint Benedict*, Chapter XXXI, written in 530 AD [See: www.ccel.org/ccel/benedict/rule2/files/rule2.html#ch31]:

> **The Cellarer**
>
> As the Cellarer of the monastery, let there be chosen from the community one who is wise, of mature character, sober, not a great eater, not haughty, not excitable, not offensive, not slow, not wasteful, but a God-fearing man who may be like a father to the whole community…
>
> Let him have charge of everything. He shall do nothing without the Abbot's orders, but keep to his instructions. Let him not vex the brethren. If any brother happens to make some unreasonable demand of him, instead of vexing the brother with a contemptuous refusal he should humbly give the reason for denying the improper request…
>
> Let him not think that he may neglect anything. He should be neither a miser nor a prodigal and squanderer of the monastery's substance, but should do all things with measure and in accordance with the Abbot's instructions…
>
> Above all things let him have humility; and if he has nothing else to give let him give a good word in answer for it is written, 'A good word is above the best gift' (Eccles. 18:17).

For 'Cellarer', read 'the modern bursar'. The chapters which follow describe these roles and responsibilities in greater detail.

Chapter 2

The all-embracing nature of the job

Richard Mayfield

What is a bursar?

The nature of the role of the bursar is changing very significantly. Never has this been more obvious to me that at this very moment, in an era in which we face constant political, financial and educational change.

Over time, the role of a bursar has become ever-more wide ranging. Historically, the experience brought to bear on the role was deeply entrenched in the military, and even today about 30% of bursars have a military background – whether directly before becoming a bursar or with some other post in between. Nowadays, however, the role is of course open to people from a much wider career spectrum and many governing bodies have realised that other skill sets and backgrounds can bring distinctively varied, but real, benefits.

I shall deploy the word 'bursars' as useful shorthand to cover school business managers, commercial managers, finance directors, heads of operations, even CFOs *et al.* (Some larger schools have created one or more of these other posts, with the holder answerable to 'the bursar'.) Whatever the person at the top of the structure is called, every one of them is integral to every decision that a business makes, whatever their degree of importance.

I use the term 'business' unapologetically, aware that some may find this offensive, preferring me to use the altogether softer and cosier word 'school'. Independent schools are *in general*, of course, quite complex organisations. Many of them exist as charities. They tread an interesting, and sometimes challenging, line in striving to balance their educational, financial and strategic aims.

But ultimately they are businesses, and in this chapter I shall concentrate on that aspect of them, and if they are not treated as such, they will cease to exist. Parents who are handing over substantial amounts of money for which they have worked extremely hard should expect – in fact, demand – that their investment is managed well. It is up to the bursar, in conjunction with the governors and the senior management team, to fulfil the duty of care to the parents.

At the very least, schools should be matching the good practices that are evident in businesses throughout the private sector. Big business, however, is afforded the luxury of being able to employ specialists. They include marketing directors; HR directors; finance directors; IT directors; press managers; social media consultants. By contrast, for the vast majority of schools many, if not all, of these functions are the responsibility of the bursar. This is why the role of the bursar has become so complex and all-embracing. The end result is a role that may well have the widest remit: all-embracing, all-encompassing.

Imagine a miracle: the bursar went home one evening, content in the knowledge that everything that could be done had, indeed, been done – and that he clearly understood everything that there was to know. By the following morning everything would have changed: such is the pace of change within the independent education sector. The role of the bursar is not for everyone. S/he gets to wear many hats. S/he must wear them all. S/he must wear them well.

Financial management and prediction

Financial management and administration has always been a core element in the role of the bursar. In its most simplistic form, this is the management of money coming into, and going out of, the business. For schools, this involves ensuring that the most potentially difficult customers (*ie* the parents) part with their hard-earned money. For most parents, school fees are their most significant outgoing, and they quite rightly demand a top-notch education.

On the expenditure side, the business of education is extremely labour intensive. Small class sizes; wide subject variety; round the clock pastoral care and well-maintained grounds and estates come at a price. With this in mind it is hardly surprising that the greatest outgoing for a school consists in paying its staff. As a rule of thumb this is likely to take 65-70% of its income.

On the income side, much of a bursar's time is, or should be, spent understanding sales. I can already hear the groans, but this aspect of the job cannot be evaded. The bursar must keep a close eye on such things as the sales mix; elasticity of demand; day to boarding ratios; the remissions policy. The last one of these is increasingly important, because it is so easy to leak money if one gets it wrong.

What is the right level of means-tested bursaries and who says so: the operators of the business, or the Charity Commission? You must decide. You must carefully analyse scholarships; forces discounts; sibling discounts; staff discounts; early payment discounts. How much should the fee increase be? What will be the impact on volume (*ie* numbers)? What comes first – the fee increase or the pay award? Questions, Questions...

What is going to happen in the next five years? Will the global recession continue? Will we have a double dip recession; inflation; stagflation; low interest rates; high interest rates; high unemployment? Uncertainty reigns in education as in all other walks of life. The school that is not looking at its long-term strategy will not exist in the long term.

All this strategic thinking sounds wonderful. However, there is also a day-to-day business to operate: having extremely difficult heartfelt discussions with parents who, owing to a change in their circumstances, can no longer afford the fees; paying suppliers; administering the payroll; negotiating with suppliers; all whilst keeping an eye on those registered, offered and accepted statistics for next year.

Ceteris paribus (all other things being equal or constant) these things are never constant. Not at our school. If you're standing still, you're going backwards. Capital projects have to be dreamed of in the first instance, then researched and reviewed *ad nauseam* and then, when the i's are dotted and the t's are crossed, it's time to pitch to the governors. Then, if you are successful and the ~~dragons~~ (sorry!) governors give the nod, the hard work really begins.

Of course, the reason that all this effort takes place is to ensure that the business makes a surplus appropriate to its needs. Many of us are the custodians of schools that have been round for many decades, if not centuries. Bursars are here to ensure that they continue to thrive. Decisions must be made for the long-term benefit of the school and not necessarily for the short-term benefit of the individuals who currently comprise it. This can cause a degree of conflict: the bursar must manage a multiplicity of individual relationships and competing interests. Yet ultimately the institution must come first.

The speed of change

The role of the bursar has changed emphatically in most schools, especially over the last decade, as its complexities have grown and accelerated. Most bursars are responsible for the finance and administration sides of the business. I myself take line management responsibilities for IT; human resources; finance and administration; catering, cleaning and maintenance; estates and grounds (including the farm); the school's equestrian enterprise and the library. This involves having a good working knowledge of an extremely wide and varied portfolio of business interests. There must be few other roles in business that involve such an umbrella of understanding.

On top of this, ICT has changed at a bewildering rate. Understanding your strategy is an extremely important element of a successful school. ICT has, and will continue, to transform how PR and marketing are delivered. How do you interact with your customers? Parents want information and they want it fast! Weekly newsletters need to be in a parents' inbox on a Monday morning: a notification needs to be sent to their mobile to tell them that it's there. Sports results and reports need to be on the web; it's the same with fixture cancellations (perish the thought).

What do your web analytics show, and how attractive is your online proposition? What social media are you embracing; what is your online policy for your students; can they access Facebook, Twitter *etc*, notwithstanding that anything you block on your server can still be viewed on their mobile phone? Then of course there's the ICT needed to deliver a modern education: hardware and software to back up the curriculum within individual subjects; to write reports; communicate with parents about day-to-day issues.

Meanwhile, a quite different set of demands faces the bursar, too. Abbotsholme is in its 121st year, so there is a huge range of buildings from different decades. Maintenance of these is no mean feat. Meetings with the site services manager happen on a daily basis. Discussions range from boiler repairs and broken windows to the arrangements for setting up a function – be it a wedding, a business conference, a concert or a fundraising event for the parents' association.

There's also the delivery of capital projects: making sure these are rigorously managed, so that those extremely reliable contractors are actually following the agreed specification that was agreed as part of the tendering process. There are also 150 acres of grounds to maintain; cricket pitches to perfect; hedges and fencing to be maintained; roads to be surfaced; windows to be washed; a minibus fleet to be managed; a sewerage plant to be maintained.

Catering presents similar challenges: making sure that Jamie Oliver would be happy if he came for lunch; dealing with special dietary requirements and nut allergies; making sure that you publish your menu a week ahead; getting 450 people through your servery each meal time; pricing items and services and ensuring that the right level of profit is achieved.

Human resources presents another rapidly growing set of demands: dealing with 140 employees and their various contract issues; drawing up coherent job descriptions and managing changes in roles; ensuring that all employees have the correct level of clearance to work in a school; advertising posts; collating applicants' details; short-listing; arranging interviews; making job offers; administering contracts and the payroll. Employment law is changing all the time and the bursar must be aware of the latest developments.

Who do bursars work with?

With so many differing roles come many different relationships, all of which require careful nurturing and management. Bursars tend to have many direct reports coming at them, from a variety of individuals. Fostering a mutually beneficial relationship with those who deliver these direct reports ensures that working at the school is both enjoyable and fulfilling for all concerned.

Weekly reviews are an absolute must if one is to stay on top of the day-to-day operations, as they facilitate the open and honest communication that is vital for the success of any business. They allow you to build the trust without which a successful team cannot operate. They must be backed with a robust system for performance management: its setting up and management are time-consuming but ultimately very rewarding for all involved. For more on this topic I recommend Patrick Lencioni's book *The Five Dysfunctions of a Team.*

However, line-managing one's own staff within the bursary is only one part of the total spectrum of relationships that a bursar must manage. S/he must also have the ability to manage and work with peers and colleagues, because the bursar is also an integral part of the school's senior management team. Within it, s/he often represents the wider view, ensuring that all decisions are fully understood and that the decisions made by the SMT are consistent with the intentions and strategy of the governing body.

In this respect above all, the relationship between the Head and the bursar is an absolutely key requisite to the future success of the school. At Abbotsholme the bursar reports to the Head, and this reporting line works well. A dysfunctional relationship between these two postholders would require a significant dose of good fortune if any school were to remain successful. Unity of purpose is important for the whole of the SMT too – so conflicting opinions should be aired and discussions should, if necessary, be extremely frank. This is healthy debate – but once the discussions are concluded and the path is chosen, the SMT must back the decision and stand as one.

Simultaneously the bursar will need to develop a strong relationship with the governing body, to help to ensure that the governors know that the school is in good hands. In some schools this relationship can be tricky at times: for example, too many governors risk becoming deeply psychologically entrenched in the history of the school, while the bursar may see the need for modernisation in an increasingly competitive arena. I am extremely lucky in this regard, but you must always be prepared: the governors quite rightly expect you to know the answers, even if they do not always find in them entirely what they want to hear.

So far I have not mentioned the most important people in the school (after the pupils, at least): the teachers. Where they are concerned, the bursar needs to recognise that his/her role is essentially a supportive one: often unsung, yet equally often indispensable. I certainly don't expect that any of the Abbotsholme pupils will remember *my* name in 20 years time, even if they remember the names of many of those who taught them. Understanding the role of the teachers; the demands they face, and which Key Stage relates to which year groups is vitally important for the bursar. It would be disrespectful not to do so. How can you ensure that a complex business is successful if you do not understand all the essential points of difference in aims, perceptions and priorities between its various types of personnel?

There are many important other relationships to consider and manage: parents (and prospective parents); pupils; the bank manager; the lawyer; the numerous contractors; the cold callers; fellow bursars; the auditors; the fire safety officer; the local council; the insurers. Thus the bursar has relationships with a very broad set of people – and a broad job to match!

A team effort

Bursars must have an extremely broad set of skills, and a wealth of experience in many different areas, if they are to add value to their school. However, this does not necessarily mean that the bursar him/herself needs to know all of the answers which are, as we have seen, changing on an almost daily basis. You need to have a great team working with you, and on whom you can rely. If the communication channels are open, and your relationships are open and honest, you have sown the seeds for being successful.

A little personal experience at this point. Bursars increasingly come from a financial background. I am a management accountant, and I believe that the operational and strategic focus that this qualification gives me is perfect for a business-focused role such as this. The broader your experience, the more likely you are to be a success. My mix of accountancy and business management roles in food manufacturing, retail, engineering, and outsourced service providing to the NHS may sound as if it indicates a somewhat zig-zag career progression, but each of these experiences has been invaluable in my current role. A new bursar with experience in only one field will experience a challenging acclimatisation.

Bursars are responsible for producing the strategy for the school in conjunction with their colleagues on the SMT – and, of course, the board. Different schools have different needs, but in general, five years is a good time-span for such an exercise. It avoids short-termism, but does not commit the school to a rigid long-term plan that cannot be adapted in the light of circumstance. Along the way, there may be different emphases – even conflict – in assessing the future. The governors' views may be different to those of the SMT – initially, at least.

It is the bursar's responsibility to bring its component parts together, in the same way in which that role falls to the finance director in any other business: it is s/he who is charged with turning these aims and objectives into a long term strategy. The bursar provides the financial reality to the Head's idealist and visionary views. Once this strategy has been approved by the governors it must be delivered both operationally and strategically.

Usually it is only the Head and the bursar who represent the views of the SMT at meetings of the full governing body – although deputies and others increasingly attend its sub-committees. As a result, it also falls to the Head and the bursar to represent the views of the governors at any subsequent meeting of the SMT. There may not always be sweetness and light in *this* gathering, either. The bursar may have to proffer an opposing view to the majority, a situation that has added piquancy when you realise that s/he is often the only person there who does not come from a teaching background. We all have our place, however, in the team and it is the multitude of different backgrounds and experiences that can be drawn on in both the management team and the governing body that offers any school the best chance of a successful future.

Thus the bursar must be able to handle difficult situations and be calm under pressure. S/he must be able to control emotions and think things through objectively. More and more focus is being placed by governors, politicians and others on the standards of the teaching profession in the widest sense, and schools are increasingly looking to the long-established performance management systems in other businesses as the mechanism to ensure they have the right teachers, behind the right desk, at the right time.

Schools will be facing exciting opportunities in this respect over the years to come – not least, in managing retirement in a post-default age era. Those that get such matters right, will thrive. Those that ignore them, or mismanage them, will have less control over their fee increases than they should have: after all, staff costs are our biggest source of expenditure.

And finally

A bursar's role is most certainly an all-encompassing one. The sheer spectrum of knowledge that you need to have is enormous. This is particularly so in smaller schools where the bursar is less likely to have specialists working for him or her in particular fields, and hence has to develop a deep understanding of each and every issue. It goes without saying that a bursar must have a strong academic record – not necessarily in the most formal sense of qualifications, but at least in having the intellectual ability to hold his or her own with academic colleagues, governors and high-powered parents. S/he will also need to have a proven track record of career experience. S/he must be an individual with a strong moral compass: someone who has the willingness and capability to live and breathe the 'brand'.

As my Headmaster says of such people: "They must walk the walk." Moreover, as someone who is likely to be making difficult and challenging decisions that may not be universally appreciated by staff, the bursar should not have a strong desire to be liked. S/he needs to be someone who is comfortable about making decisions solely because s/he knows that they are in the best interests of the school.

In the past bursars were known as being authoritarian: people who ran things with a strong arm. This is no longer the case. Leading bursars have the skills to get the best out of their employees, through coaching, mentoring or the management of capability. They are leaders in the true sense – but this cannot be at the expense of being a highly effective team player within the SMT. They need to be confident, unafraid of being questioned and able to justify important decisions.

A more challenging, wide ranging role would be difficult to find in any business. As I sit at my desk writing this, overlooking the Roseyard, with pupils heading to their first lesson of the day after the harvest festival has finished in our beautiful chapel, I look at my diary for today: weekly reviews with the IT manager, finance manager and HR manager; a parent who has fallen on hard times; a family that is interested in our wedding facilities; those who attend the pre-year-end audit meeting; with the parents' association committee; then, a business enterprise lesson with Year 9 at the end of the day. Nothing strange there: every day is different, and as a bursar the only consistent part of the role is the inconsistency.

That is why the role of the bursar is so rewarding and provides such great job satisfaction. I love my job. Our product is fantastic and we will continue to improve it. My role is to ensure that our stakeholders can continue to enjoy Abbotsholme in the same way that others have for the last 121 years.

Chapter 3

The bursar and the bursarial team

Annika Hedrich-Wiggans

The bursar's role is, by its very nature, highly varied. It contains some degree of unpredictability. While this can – and does – lead to stressful times and situations, it is also an important contributing factor in making the role so fulfilling. However, in order to cope with the unpredictability, pressures and fast-paced life, it is crucially important to ensure that an adequate internal support network is established to assist the bursar, so that pressure points and unexpected problems do not impact on the quality of day-to-day support services provided to the school.

I try to keep reminding my governors, the Head and perhaps most crucially, the teaching staff, of the importance of high standards of administration and support services in any independent school. I strongly believe these are a key factor in ensuring a school's success, development and long term survival.

The bursar's PA

A top-class PA/secretary will be essential for most bursars. Such a person must take on a sufficient proportion of the considerable day-to-day administrative workload for the bursar to feel confident that delegated tasks are carried out efficiently and to a high standard. Having got the appointment wrong a couple of times, I came to realise just how important it is to get this right: it is worth investing money in advertisements and devoting time to a thorough recruitment process.

Many bursars will encounter highly sensitive issues and information at regular intervals whilst in post, and this applies particularly to those who also combine their role with that of clerk to the governors. Discretion will be a key quality to look for in the bursar's PA, and a high-quality PA will not only be of great assistance to the bursar in difficult times, but will also relish the variety and challenges that come with such an important post.

The finance team

The size and composition of a school's finance function clearly varies, depending on the size and nature of each particular school and its requirements. That aside, there appears to remain amongst some people an old-fashioned perception of 'The Bursary', consisting of one-and-a-half persons, huddled in a dark back room over handwritten ledgers. It is an important task for any bursar to remind governors of the importance of adequate manpower, proper staff qualifications and sufficient investment into the right accounting systems – and to have trust in those governors with business/commercial expertise to support the argument!

Some schools, particularly smaller ones, may choose to outsource certain aspects of their accounts function, the most frequent example being the preparation of the annual statutory accounts. It is, however, crucial in my view to have at least one professionally-qualified accountant in the in-house team, if day-to-day accounting procedures and financial controls are to be implemented effectively. I have encountered several schools (typically, smaller ones) that lack quite basic processes such as the preparation of regular management accounts; the setting and monitoring of financial policies *etc.* Reliance on external auditors or other financial advisers is insufficient to ensure the effective financial management which can only work well if driven from within the school.

The financially-trained person does not necessarily have to be the bursar, although s/he should possess a good level of financial awareness and a genuine interest in financial matters. This appointment can simply be of the 'school accountant' variety: one of the best of these with whom I have ever worked trained whilst in post to obtain an AAT qualification. This gave us a combination of up-to-date practical book-keeping skills on her part and a (slightly faded) ACA qualification on mine. It worked extremely well.

Recruitment opportunities in my current school have led to the appointment of three AAT/ACCA qualified bursary staff, in addition to the ACA-qualified bursar and the finance bursar. The calibre of staff that

I was able to recruit as a result of stipulating the necessity for a qualification is, I believe, much higher than it would have been had we advertised for non-qualified staff.

It also gives the finance bursar greater scope for delegating certain tasks and projects, particularly at pressure points throughout the financial year. It is worth casting a wide net when recruiting: I have, for example, known former high street bank staff who adapted brilliantly to their new roles in the bursary, and it is my conclusion that having already had experience in schools should not necessarily be a major requirement in the appointment decision.

Buildings

While larger schools have greater requirements than those that are smaller, it can also easily be appreciated that, compared to day schools, most buildings-related issues in any boarding school are of much greater priority, because pupil and staff safety and welfare have so many additional aspects.

However, at the very least every school should have a rolling remedial works schedule in order to ensure that all parts of its site are maintained. It is much more difficult (from a practical and financial point of view) to catch up with building work once progress has been allowed to fall behind schedule, than it is to keep continually upgrading. The cosmetic appearance of a school also remains an important marketing tool (possibly more so to parents than pupils), and whilst it may be tempting to cut investment into maintenance works when finances are tight, this really should be a last resort: a school that *looks* like a struggling school will soon *become* a struggling school.

I do not think that any school, even a small day school, should try to survive without at least one reasonably well-trained and enthusiastic workman. One school I knew that attempted to do so had a bursary that was overwhelmed with perpetual low-level requests from the teachers and pupils alike ('broken' radiators that weren't turned on; lost pupil locker keys *etc*). This led not only to on-going interruptions to the finance staff, but also to understandable frustration amongst the teachers when requests were not addressed quickly.

What most agitates members of the school community is a lack of progress in relation to small, remedial repairs. Their perception of the quality of the site as a whole will suddenly be much better if they observe the basics being addressed efficiently on a day-to-day basis. The conclusion is therefore inescapable: sufficient and easily accessible manpower must be available to do the work. When planning new building projects, it is also important to remember that those new buildings will need to be maintained: an expanded site will require an extended maintenance team.

On the other hand, external contractors also have their place and merits. Consider this in the context of an in-house painter, working whilst pupils are present. Any indoor work in public areas will require the tidying up of equipment before each break, and setting up again afterwards; some areas may require careful fencing off and others may be completely out of bounds. Supervision of that painter can also become a problem, as indeed can levels of motivation and speed of work, given the monotony of the tasks involved.

As a result of all these considerations, a bursar may well find that use of reliable external contractors during school holidays is a more efficient solution that provides value for money and minimises disruption during term time. The web-based ISBA members' noticeboard is a useful starting point for obtaining details of recommended specialist suppliers for such contract services.

Other areas of work in which external contractors can be used effectively are those that are tightly regulated, such as gas and electricity. For many schools, employing suitably-qualified engineers and electricians is simply not an option from a financial point of view, and the on-going cost of staff maintaining their qualifications is also considerable.

There is, however, merit in involving in-house staff in projects where cabling and pipe work are installed, even if they are not the persons carrying out the direct works. It will give them a level of knowledge that may well facilitate on-going maintenance work once a building project is completed. An additional benefit is that this can also give them a more tangible sense of 'ownership' of a new build or major refurbishment.

The exact structure of each maintenance department will vary from school to school. In some, an estates bursar, possibly assisted by a deputy and a clerk of works, will head up a major in-house team that may also manage major new building projects in-house. In others, a simple foreman or caretaker may suffice. Whatever the exact skills set and qualifications that are needed in a particular school, my experience is that recruiting the head of department from outside the organisation can work better than promoting from inside. There seems to exist a degree of difficulty for those who are seen to have 'come up through the tools' to assert the necessary level of authority in what can be a complex department.

Grounds and gardens

Grounds and gardens may be maintained by one combined or two separate teams, depending on the size of campus. At my present school, the two teams have historically been separate but are now being combined under the head groundsman's management. My thinking behind this is to improve the efficiency of both teams, as a result of them being better placed to combine forces in busy periods. They can also undertake joint major landscaping projects during the quieter winter months.

Perhaps the groundsman's greatest challenge is to cope with the on-going demands from users of the sports pitches, particularly if these are also rented out to external users during holiday periods. He has the difficult task of ensuring that the maximum number of pupils are given opportunities to play sport (which will be the forceful argument from any sports department), whilst also protecting – and ideally improving – the quality of surfaces and soil conditions. His relationship with the director of sport may therefore not be without friction, and he may need the bursar's support from time to time in his discussions.

Catering

I have worked with in-house catering teams at schools, as well as catering services that were either fully or partly outsourced to contractors. In my experience, the kitchen staff's loyalties lie with the school, irrespective of whether or not they are technically employed by an external organisation.

There may be merit in outsourcing just the staff employment and food hygiene/food safety aspects to a contractor. Kitchens are often stressful working environments that can nurture tensions amongst employees; they also tend to be staffed by lower-skilled workers with potentially high staff turnover. From a health and safety aspect, catering is a high-risk activity. All these reasons combined may make outsourcing an attractive option, particularly in schools with no dedicated HR function or health and safety officer

Where outsourcing does affect day-to-day catering significantly is in the area of purchasing and, specifically, in the school's ability to choose suppliers. When working in the West Country, for example, my school wanted to take advantage of the excellent local produce available. This proved to be impossible as long as our purchasing arrangements were outsourced and eventually led to a decision to move all purchasing in-house. We found that, as a result, the quality of the ingredients supplied to the school improved dramatically, and we even discovered that some prices were lower!

The bursar will have to work closely with the catering manager to ensure that internal catering issues and more formal entertaining are kept under control. How quickly a requirement for basic refreshments for a particular event can escalate into a three-course meal with wine! Catering managers, if they are ambitious and take pride in their work, can sometimes be their own worst enemy in this process. It will be important for the bursar to review the scale and cost of catering functions regularly and if necessary to remind colleagues that first and foremost – particularly in a boarding school – the quality of core pupil feeding must not be compromised.

Housekeeping (cleaning and porters)

By nature an area that is characterised by high-turnover, low-skilled and low-earning staff, each school will have its own arrangements for housekeeping services. Whether it is outsourced or managed in house, adequate supervision of staff is of key importance. Staff timekeeping is a recurring problem, as is the challenge to keep standards of cleaning at a consistently high level.

Unfortunately (unless I have just been unlucky), the necessity for disciplinary meetings with staff will arise from time to time. It is therefore important to ensure that the member of staff responsible for cleaners' supervision (occasionally someone who may have risen through the ranks) undergoes training in human resources management and is aware of the facts of basic employment law. It is also important that the bursar (or personnel manager, if applicable) is sufficiently aware of any staff-related changes, developments or problems from the outset, in order to ensure that all necessary processes are followed.

Personnel

Legislation affecting independent schools has increased in volume and complexity in recent years. I am not simply referring to direct regulations such as those issued by Ofsted, ISI and others, but possibly even more so the pitfalls of employment law – and all these changes have taken place within the context of an increased litigious culture amongst the public in general.

In my current school, and for the first time ever as a bursar, I am fortunate to work with a dedicated personnel manager. Without doubt she not only significantly lightens my everyday workload, but also provides a well-qualified and reasoned sounding board for human resources-related issues as they appear. It would be unrealistic to assume that the majority of bursars will be in a similar position and therefore all should aim to obtain a reasonable knowledge of HR and employment law. It is also helpful to identify a reliable and reasonably priced firm of solicitors who can assist with problems as they arise. It is important that the bursar knows whom to approach with minor, yet potentially important, legal queries.

It is crucial to ensure that processes related to staff recruitment are followed by the ISI/Ofsted book: in particular that the Central Register of Appointments is kept up-to-date. This in itself will constitute a considerable proportion of a bursar's (or personnel manager's) workload.

Health and safety

I encourage any bursar to appoint a dedicated health and safety officer, if it is at all financially possible. This does not have to be a full-time post; indeed my current (large) school is served by a part-timer. The crucial requirement is to employ a person with no other responsibilities, someone who can devote sufficient time to fulfilling paperwork requirements;

dealing with problems and emergencies as they arise, and keeping abreast of changing legislation.

It is also important for the bursar to communicate to all staff that a health and safety officer cannot be 'responsible for' health and safety. The responsibility must lie with *all* staff, and school inspectors in particular like to see evidence of this. They are impressed to see, for example, that individual house-parents take on full responsibility for fire drills in their house. The health and safety officer's responsibility is to ensure that all requirements under health and safety legislation are met, and that staff are sufficiently trained to achieve this. The role therefore is one of administrator, co-ordinator and monitor.

The health and safety officer can by nature be a highly unpopular role, and if it is going to be successful, recruiting a person with the right personality for it is crucial. Whilst specific requirements will vary from school to school: the appointment of a retired senior housemaster has worked extremely well at my school. He not only has the in-depth understanding of the school site and its operations, but also the long-established respect from staff across the campus that makes it easy to achieve his goals. A great sense of humour also helps!

And finally, some practical points

Space constraints for administration offices can be a real problem in an environment in which attention focuses on the provision of core services: in this case, teaching and possibly boarding. The layout of rooms and buildings that were originally designed for another purpose can also present problems, and in extreme cases they may not be fit for purpose. My own school's work spaces have included a former classroom next to an assembly hall; a gatekeeper's lodge; a converted basement changing room and a residential town house. Some work better than others!

My key objective is to select a location and a space that ensures two things. On the one hand, that those members of bursary staff who are key 'front of house' people from the viewpoint of parents, teachers and pupils are easily accessible in a location that is easily reached and accessible within the school.

On the other hand members of finance staff in particular need to have sufficient quiet time without interruptions. Some bursaries work around this problem by restricting opening hours, something that I personally do not favour. A successful alternative solution for me has been an early start time for staff; the use of flexitime (*ie* so that staff start or finish work in quiet times of day) and ensuring that bursary staff share sufficient knowledge for any one of them to answer standard queries.

It is important for all other support staff heads of department to be situated where their staff are – for instance the catering manager next to the kitchens. It is therefore even more important for the bursar to leave sufficient time to visit those satellite locations as frequently as necessary: the bursar's day-to-day job is highly unlikely ever to be a purely office-based one.

And when all is said and done, never underestimate the importance of professional development training for bursary personnel. There are obvious training opportunities for the bursar – for example in the shape of excellent ISBA-organised events. However, it can be more difficult to identify training needs and solutions for members of the bursar's team. A system of regular staff appraisals is an important tool to help identify gaps in knowledge and scope for professional development, and this then prompts both the member of staff and the bursar to look out for relevant training courses.

Chapter 4

An introductory guide to child protection

Nigel Richardson

In nearly all schools, the bulk of the pastoral work – including child protection (CP) (also known as 'safeguarding', and closely linked to requirements for Safer Recruitment) – falls on the teaching staff rather than on the bursar and the bursary team. Tutors and form teachers see children day-to-day and are watchful for any concerns that they may have: house-parents or pastoral section heads, pastoral deputies, the Head him/herself deal with the more significant cases, depending on what appears to be their level of seriousness and/or the balance of likelihoods.

Normally there is a senior member of the teaching staff who is the designated child protection (CP) officer, with a role that includes liaison with the local authority (LA) child protection team, and two-yearly refresher training. All staff – including non-teaching/support staff – are expected to receive appropriate induction on arrival, and further updates every three years.

All schools should have their main procedures set out in the staff handbook, and clear policies in place that include a statement of the process whereby allegations will be investigated. These policies should be on a school's website, and the key documentation should be approved by governors at least once a year. A member of the governing body is normally designated as the CP governor, and charged with an annual review of the policies; of cases dealt with and how the school's responsibilities have been carried out.

LAs and the various independent schools' professional associations provide in-service courses, and specialist lawyers advise on the documentation. With CP now so firmly established as a priority in every school, and with the Independent Schools Inspectorate (ISI) having been in existence for two decades, any incoming bursar should find that a school has the required policies in place already, requiring annual updating rather than compiling from first principles.

All that said, however, the bursarial staff have a specific and vitally important part to play in the CP process. In most schools, it is the bursar whose department is responsible for the process of carrying out criminal and other checks on would-be teachers and support staff; for the keeping of sound records and for the maintenance of a central register of appointments' checks which will be scrutinised as part of the inspection process. It may also fall to the bursar (particular if s/he is also clerk to the governors) to be the person designated in the child protection policy to take the first steps in the event of any complaint against the Head.

It is also very important to remember that sometimes it is support staff and volunteers (perhaps helping with reading in class), rather than teachers, who are the first people in whom a child confides. The school nurse; the person in the bursary dealing with pupils' lost locker keys; the friendly caretaker or groundsman: all these people need training in how to spot the signs, or how to respond to allegations and confidences offered, and this should be an integral part of the training of *all* bursary staff.

Appropriate guidance should also be included in the support staff handbook, reflecting both the fact that support staff are *not* from a teaching background (and thus probably less aware of how CP good practice must shape all their actions), and that there is likely to be a different context to most of the potentially difficult situations that they may encounter. As a result, one should tailor-make such guidance (and the training that goes with it), avoiding the temptation simply to cut and paste from the teaching staff handbook.

Despite all this, one still hears from time to time of schools that have been found wanting, so it is worth reminding ourselves of how and why the contemporary preoccupation with all these procedures has come about. It was not always so.

Child protection is a multi-faceted concept. It embraces such areas as pupil health and safety; bullying; medical needs and first aid; school security and drugs and substance misuse. However in the popular consciousness it has come to centre on the cruel treatment (psychological, as well as physical) and above all the sexual abuse of children.

Sadly the problem is not new. Over many years, in an unknown number of schools of all types – day as well as boarding, maintained as well as independent, senior as well as junior – a small proportion of staff mistreated children. (This is, of course, an underlying theme in many fictional writings, too.) The first significant Act of Parliament for the Prevention of Cruelty to Children was passed as long ago as 1889, and there was periodic new legislation throughout the 20th century.

However, until fairly recently it tended to centre on problems within families, or in connection with children in foster care, or those living under the supervision of social services. In 1974, the death of Maria Colwell at the hands of her stepfather highlighted the lack of coordination amongst services that oversaw child welfare: the pre-occupations and emphasis began to change as a result.

From the end of the 1980s, the speed of change dramatically increased – particular with regard to schools, and notably with the Children Act, 1989. Its main principle was that *all* children should be protected from harm; it, and the investigation by Esther Rantzen and her BBC TV *That's Life* team into the appalling state of affairs at Crookham Court boarding school (1991) led to major new demands on schools in terms of the facilities provided for their pupils.

All schools were required to provide private 24-hour phoning-out facilities for boarders. Childline was born, and with it a system of external listeners whom children could contact: schools were required to display posters advertising the existence of these innovations. As a prep school Head at that time, I had to oversee one of the first trials of pupil questionnaires compiled by the Oxfordshire LA, covering a wide variety of issues about their daily lives and the adults whom they encountered.

The Care Standards Act and the National Minimum Standards for Boarding followed within a decade – along with far stricter requirements on the inspection of boarding care. The demands for further legislation became much more urgent in the wake of a series of new tragedies –

again, mostly involving children not in the context of school: Jasmine Beckford and Victoria Climbié, to name just two.

But in August 2002 the murders of two schoolgirls in Soham, Cambridgeshire, by caretaker Ian Huntley, a trusted member of his local school community, showed the inadequacy of the existing DfE *List 99* and other checks on adults working in schools.

From those terrible events, a stream of Inquiries (notably Bichard, and later Laming and Singleton) and further regulation followed – including CRB checks and the highly detailed Early Years Foundation Stage welfare requirements for the youngest school children. Safer recruitment procedures were introduced, including wording to be included in advertisements about a school's commitment to CP; standard application forms and interview panel training.

In the final years of the Labour government of 1997-2010, the Safeguarding of Children Act 2006 paved the way for a new Vetting and Barring Scheme run by an Independent Safeguarding Authority whose remit would include even occasional volunteers working in schools. It was estimated that well over 10m people would be drawn into this system and some (notably authors visiting schools on a one-off basis to talk about the books they had written) protested that this constituted an infringement of other liberties, as well as being a disproportionate response to the problem.

The full range of requirements in force in 2009-10 was described in volume 5 in this series, *Pastoral Work and Those who Practise It*, chapter 2: 'Pastoral Issues and the Law' by Sue Freestone.

The coalition government's election victory in 2010 brought with it new questions about practicality, affordability (both to the government administering the schemes and to individual schools paying fees for checks) and new calls for proportionality – as well as a new political approach with possible new priorities, yet to be determined. A series of reviews of different aspects of CP was launched – including issues around vetting and barring, the processing of checks and their subsequent portability.

Early in 2011 it was announced that the vetting and barring scheme would be scaled down – particularly in its application to occasional and/or voluntary personnel in schools.

The full extent to which the whole process has mushroomed was highlighted in Professor Eileen Munro's first report: 'Analysis of the Problems'. This states (paragraph 1.8):

> Professionals working with children and young people in social care, health, education, and police services have access to detailed guidance and procedures to inform the way they work together to safeguard children and young people. Parton (Parton, N. (2010), The Increasing Complexity of 'Working Together to Safeguard Children in England') reports that the first formulation of Government guidance in 1974 was seven pages long, whilst the latest statutory guidance, published in 2010, has 390 pages and makes references to ten other pieces of supplementary guidance that provide a further 424 pages.

All of this makes it impossible to go into prescriptive detail in this book: things change very fast and are currently in a state of flux. In the years ahead, ISBA will be able to advise bursars on websites and other sources of information about the requirements and regulations currently in force. Meanwhile, however, it is worth remembering two key things.

First, in philosophical terms, great advances have been made in recent decades in the protection of children. We have a moral duty to do all we can to protect children of all ages. We have become more child-centred in our thinking; more prepared to recognise that children, as well as adults, have rights; that they deserve to be treated with respect and to be free from fear and danger.

Whatever the current practical issues and costs – and the absurdities that over-zealous application of rules may have thrown up in the past, it is now much harder than it once was for evil adults to prey on vulnerable children, or for staff known to be suspect to be quietly passed on from one school to another. Yet no system is foolproof and we should never be complacent.

Secondly, child protection rightly remains a topic of great concern to the public at large – including the parents in our schools. The press takes a big interest in it, too. No school is more at risk in reputational terms than one that adopts a cavalier attitude to CP – especially if it is caught out by parents or inspectors and then subsequently tries to cover things up.

These two considerations make many practical demands on us. These include (see chapter 10) the requirement for a 'safer recruitment' trained member on interview panels. We need to be aware of many issues relating to parental responsibility in respect, for example, of separated families. Who has legal responsibility? Do any court orders apply? Who pays the fees? Who is entitled to information? Do I have the subject's authority to divulge records or information, to the police or any other institutional body? An increasing number of schools follow hospital guidelines in this respect.

Finally, the detailed mechanics of child protection – its checks, records and registers – are never going to be undemanding or glamorous. However, keeping up-to-date with them and administering them effectively is one of the most important aspects of the way in which the bursary team supports the work of a school – and of the people who work in it, whether as teachers or taught.

Chapter 5

Policy statements and the rolling review

Mike Vacher

Definition

Policy: 1. A course or principle of action adopted or proposed by a government, party, business or individual *etc.* 2. Prudent conduct; sagacity.

The Concise Oxford Dictionary (Eighth Edition)

Overview and requirement

School policies are part of the essential bureaucracy that provides for, and demonstrates, the formal regulation of the establishment. In schools which are charities (and many others that are not), policies support the objects and mission statement by providing the framework on which the routine management and functions of the school are based. Good practice in this area helps to ensure that the statutory requirements are met, and to enable efficient administration and management of the school to take place.

Schools are under twin obligations in respect of policies: first, to have those that the law requires and, indeed, others which, for practical reasons, may be highly desirable. Secondly, they must ensure that those that fall into the legally required category are regularly reviewed by the governing body. While the board may choose to delegate its reviewing *function* to a sub-committee or other group, it cannot delegate its *powers*: board members are individually and collectively responsible for the finished version(s).

Thus the policies themselves can be divided into two categories:

- Those that are a legal requirement.

- Others that provide specific guidance as required by the governors, the senior management team (SMT) or some other body or group that is responsible for the affairs of the school, to ensure that the school is run in accordance with good practice and the governors' strategic intentions.

Legally required policies

These are statutory or regulatory, and are assessed by the Independent Schools Inspectorate (ISI). They are usefully explained in the ISI *Handbook for the Inspection of Schools – The Regulatory Requirements*. It is usually updated termly, and is available on the ISI website.

Template examples of these ISI regulatory policies are available on the ISBA website at: www.theisba.org.uk/frameset_m.asp?l=/home.asp? They are available to schools not in membership of the ISBA by contacting the ISBA office: Tel: 01256 330369.

These compulsory policies are:

- Statement of ethos and aims.
- Curriculum.
- Admissions.
- Admissions and attendance register.
- Scheme of work for Personal, Social and Health Education (PSHE).
- Anti-bullying.
- Safeguarding and welfare of children.
- Health and safety on school trips.
- Behaviour, discipline, sanctions and exclusions.
- Risk assessments for the workplace and away from school.
- Fire risk policy and assessment.
- Fire procedures and arrangements.
- First aid.
- Arrangements for the supervision of students.
- Central appointments register.
- Three year plan for meeting Special Educational Needs and Disability Act (SENDA) requirements – including information about English as an Additional Language.

- Complaints procedure.
- Contact details of the school, Head and proprietor/chairman of governors.

School policies

Governors and the SMT will also wish to have in place sufficient additional policies to ensure the smooth running of their school. It is possible that a school will have a veritable library of policies covering the whole range of functions. Some might affect comparatively few members of the community; others are fundamental to all. They may range from the stratospherically important to the comparatively mundane, and they usefully cover such matters as the 'appraisal of the SMT' or 'pupil attendance at parties policy'.

Occasionally, however, the presence of the more unusual directives in a school's list might reflect a 'hiccup' in that specific area in which expectations of normal common sense were dumbfounded by an alarming chain of events that resulted in a cry of: "We must write a policy to ensure it does not happen again."

The number and type of school policies will depend on the circumstances of the school, and they vary according to each establishment. Many will simply be a policy statement and it is usual for many of these school policies to be swept up in the staff, parent or pupil handbooks. The following might be included:

- Adults living in boarding accommodation (required under national minimum standards)
- Absence due to sickness or injury
- Appraisal of SMT
- Capability, discipline and grievance procedures
- Code of conduct
- Common room handbook
- Community handbook (including pupil joining instructions)
- Data protection policy
- Discipline policy
- Domestic incident leave

- Drugs and substance abuse
- Emergency action and disaster recovery plan
- End of employment procedure
- Equal opportunities policy
- Expenses policy
- Flexible working policy
- Gifted and talented policy
- Grievance procedure
- Health promotion policy
- Homework policy
- Induction programme for teachers new to the school
- Induction programme for NQTs
- Induction training of governors
- Induction training for support staff
- Initial teacher training policy
- Intellectual property rights
- IT/internet acceptable use policy
- Laptop policy and loan agreement
- Marking and assessment policy
- Maternity leave policy
- Missing child plan
- Pandemic flu policy
- Parental leave policy
- Paternity leave scheme
- Policy for monitoring by board of governors of welfare provision for boarders
- Procedure for the conduct by the governors of reviews and appeals
- Pupil attendance at parties policy
- Recruitment of ex-offenders and security of disclosure information
- Retirement procedure
- School rules
- Service occupancy policy
- Staff professional development
- Standing financial instructions

- Support staff appraisal
- Teacher appraisal
- Whistle-blowing policy
- Working time regulations

Schools should check this list with their lawyer from time to time, to see which policies s/he regards as being legal requirements or good practice, in terms of employment law. It is always as well to be fully up-to-date and, ideally, ahead of the game.

Governors also need to ensure that there are sufficient additional policies to give them confidence that the school is being administered technically in accordance with their intent. Thus there may be additional policies for:

- Award of scholarships and bursaries
- Debtors' management and late payment of fees
- Reserves policy
- Investment policy
- Delegations – financial and other
- Decisions reserved for governors: *eg* appointment of Head and bursar
- Risk management
- Conflicts of interest
- SMT salaries

Practicalities

A school's policies must be all embracing and must provide for the efficient running of the establishment. However, there is a balance to be struck in establishing the framework. Some organisations will seek to insure against any eventuality by providing a directive – and will then sit back in the confidence that everything is in order, almost certainly to discover that some once-in-a-millennium freak accident or exceptional piece of pupil misbehaviour disrupts the false sense of security. Others choose to adopt a minimalist approach by holding as few policies as possible. Whatever, it is essential that:

- A school's polices meet the statutory and regulatory requirements

- There is an established process for reviewing, updating and approving them

All staff must know:

- What the policies contain
- Where they can be found
- Those policies they must have a working knowledge of, and those that can be used for reference
- Those policies that are public (and in particular available to parents), and those that are only for internal use

Responsibilities – the 'policy on policies'

The governors have ultimate responsibility for ensuring that all *statutory and regulatory* requirements are being met and implemented, and (as already explained) this cannot ultimately be delegated to others. Thus it is essential that effective monitoring and evaluation mechanisms are in place.

In addition, Heads and bursars have responsibility for advising governors of the scope and content of *all* policies and ensuring that they are implemented with appropriate instruction and training provided. Staff members have responsibility for knowing and carrying out the direction contained in school policies once these have been brought to their attention.

Governors may wish to set out the mechanisms by which all these responsibilities are discharged. This might lead them to request a 'policy on policies' that details the methods of accountability, review, amendment and promulgation. An example of a simple version is included at the end of this chapter.

The policy process

Drafting: responsibility for individual policies is often allocated to members of the SMT or individual members of staff. It must, however, be appreciated that some policies overlap, and it is therefore helpful if policies are drafted in the same format and make reference to other, related policies. As already stated, authoritative templates for the core policies are now available on the ISBA website. These template policies are reviewed by the appropriate professional advisers including the ISI;

therefore if followed, schools can be confident that their policies will comply with the standard required.

It is important, however, that each school ensures that policies meet their specific needs and address the practicalities of carrying out any directives stated within them. It is helpful to provide room for some flexibility, but ambiguity should be avoided.

On the other hand, policies that are too prescriptive risk being cast aside and left unused, or consistently not adhered to. Policies should be kept concise and in clear and straightforward language. This can be helped by providing an overarching statement or frontispiece, with details covered in annexes and appendices whenever appropriate.

Approval: it is helpful if a formal process for the approval of policies is followed. Core policies – such as those covering admissions, child protection, complaints and health and safety – must be seen and approved by governors, and the fact that this has taken place should be recorded in the minutes of their meetings.

Those policies which are more to do with the day-to-day management of the school might be approved by the SMT. However, governors need to retain an overarching responsibility for policies and, taken to an extreme, there is an argument that they should review every policy. Such diligence would, however, prevent governors from attending to more strategic matters and would result in much of their meetings focusing on minutiae and phraseology.

Nevertheless, it is very helpful if one or more governors can take responsibility for overseeing certain policy areas or even agreeing to act as lead for all policy matters. This enables the process to be streamlined with reports summarising progress being tabled routinely at governors' meetings. This might be in tabular format such as shown below:

Review: in order to maintain their currency, policies need to be kept under continual periodic review. The most important polices (child protection, health and safety and risk management) are required to be formally reviewed by governors annually. Others can be left for longer, but it should be remembered that leaders (as in the table above) ought to be keeping their own policies under continual review within an overall

Title	Date of last approval	Most recent update	Current status	Lead governor	Lead SMT executive	Date of next review

programme. Governors should be routinely presented with a report to demonstrate the latest situation with all policies.

Amendments: the 'master' copy of each policy should be regularly updated by the lead person, when and as appropriate. Now that the ISBA has provided a template it can be assumed that notice of important changes brought about by adjustment and updating of statutory directions will be publicised from time to time and these updates should trigger amendments to school policies by the appropriate lead person. However, it is important that schools do not develop an over-reliance on the ISBA and they should carry out their own due diligence.

Promulgation: updated policies need to be endorsed by governors (when appropriate) and promulgated across the school community. A robust plan is required to ensure that all members of it, governors, staff, parents and pupils, know of the policies relevant to them. Some schools choose to adopt an open and transparent approach by publishing all policies on the school website. Conversely, this can lack focus; it can provide a list that few will study in detail, and potentially risks giving away good ideas to local competitors! Under the current regulations only the child protection policy is required to be held on the school website (if the school has a website).

Others can be summarised or referred to in a school handbook or included in the staff handbook(s). Wherever a school decides to publish its policies, the key point is ensuring that it is readily accessible to the relevant areas of the school community. It may be considered good practice to obtain written acknowledgement on an annual basis, or at least during induction, that members of staff have received, read and understood key documents and policies.

Training: staff training must include reference to the school's policies, both during induction and on a regular basis. There are advantages in providing a policy update routinely during the school year and, for example, ensuring that policy changes are a regular item on meeting agendas, in order to drip-feed information to staff to cascade down to others.

* * * *

Policy on policies

Here is an example of such a document:

Principles

1. Responsibility for policies lies with the governing body.
2. Responsibility for the timely production of the policies lies with the Head and bursar.
3. The senior management team shall be tasked by the governing body through the Head and bursar to review policies on a regular basis (see below).
4. The Head/bursar shall inform the senior management team of any changes, statutory or otherwise, to any policy and when the changes take effect.
5. The senior management team shall then review the policy regardless of the place of the policy in the review process.
6. All policies shall be published on the website/intranet except when decided otherwise.
7. Each policy shall have a title page including a policy statement encapsulating the nature of the policy, the date of drafting/approval and the date of next review.
8. All policies shall be written to make accessing and understanding them, and using them for rapid reference, as easy as possible. To this end, pages and sections should be numbered.

Reviewing policies

9. The risk assessment policy shall be reviewed annually by the governors (a statutory requirement).
10. The standing financial instructions shall be reviewed annually under the direction of the finance and general purpose committee.
11. The health and safety policy shall be reviewed annually by the health and safety committee and approved by the governors as a statutory requirement.
12. The child protection policy shall be reviewed annually by governors.
13. All other policies shall be reviewed every two years on a rolling programme as coordinated by the bursar.

Chapter 6

Strategic planning; finance and budgeting issues; presenting accounts

Yvonne Thomas

There was a time when a school was a school, and the Head and the bursar were generally at war – the Head being a thoughtless spendthrift, and the bursar a visionless miser. They joined forces only in order to outwit the short-sighted governors. Those days are gone: we cannot allow ourselves to drift into those caricatures. Schools are businesses: most of them complex businesses. Heads, bursars and governors need to find an effective way to work together.

Governors can add a more balanced view of matters to which the Head and bursar are too close, and can also offer informed advice from their particular career specialisms. However, they have appointed the Head and bursar to lead the management of the business, and they need to allow the space for that to happen.

The remit of the bursar has always included responsibility for co-coordinating the school finances, but over recent years the adoption of a wider professional approach has become vital. The mounting complexity of charity accounting requirements; close scrutiny by bankers; public benefit requirements, and the adverse economic conditions combine to make financial skills essential within the bursary. If the bursar does not have the necessary expertise, an accountant is a vital member of the bursary team, if resources allow. If not, financial help will be needed from external accountants or the auditors.

In using the term 'bursar', I include any person who is responsible for the finance, administration and operations side of the school, *ie* generally the bits that are not actually *teaching*. It does not matter whether the title is bursar, operations director, business manager or controller of resources *etc*: it is the professionalism with which your remit is performed that matters. So, if you are not an accountant, you still need to gain enough knowledge to be able to understand the basics of your school's accounts: the task of accounts' preparation can be delegated, but not the ultimate responsibility. There is plenty of training available, with a good general introduction being included on the ISBA course for new bursars.

It is the responsibility of a bursar to co-ordinate the school finances, but not to be the sole guardian. Effective financial management must be a team effort, with the Head, bursar and senior managers all buying into the current plan, whether it be for retrenchment, consolidation or expansion. Mixed messages will unsettle the school and confuse the governors.

Many schools have a finance or finance and general purposes committee to take a detailed look at finance papers in advance of the main board meetings. A close working relationship with the chairman of finance is also a necessity, particularly if the bursar's main area of professional expertise does not lie in the area of finance.

The following notes are written with a practical rather than technical approach and include basic points for those with a limited financial experience.

The financial cycle

The management of the finances is an iterative process, sometimes called the 'financial cycle' (see figure 1 opposite).

Budgeting

The agreement of a realistic yet challenging budget is the first step in the process of efficient financial control. The chances are that you will join a school part-way through the year, after the budget has been set. This is probably no bad thing, as you will have time to study the shortcomings of your predecessor's figures before having to present your own ideas. Do not waste this opportunity to study the figures in detail, and pay particular attention to major variances.

The annual budget will need to be prepared within the context of the school strategic or development plan, which most schools now have in

Figure 1 – the financial cycle

one format or another – indeed it is now part of the (huge) pack of paperwork required by inspectors. So, if you do not already have one, add it to the urgent list.

Authority levels

A clear and widely publicised list of authorised budget holders and ordering procedures is essential for budget management. If one exists already, review it – and then check that it is actually complied with. If one does not yet exist, draw up a suggested draft for discussion with the Head and chairman of finance.

Of course, even having clear guidelines will not necessarily stop a rogue staff member or even a Head in full cry from falling off the wagon (or buying something that did exactly that), but at least there will be something to brandish 'more in sorrow than in anger' afterwards. And if this happens to you, take some comfort at being in good company. I list below some examples given when a few bursars compared notes in the bar at an ISBA conference some years ago:

The Head had always fancied having an amphitheatre in the field behind the school. While the bursar was away, a contractor called at the school gate with several lorry-loads of hard core, available very cheaply. The Head saw a marvellous opportunity and accepted delivery for 'cash in hand' to the unknown contractor. Upon his return the bursar had to pay to have the materials removed, as there was no evidence of the source and suitability of the materials.

A receptionist ordered a ten-year supply of franking machine labels, because the price per box was such a bargain. The boxes are still almost filling the stock room and there can be no question of upgrading the franking machine, because such an action would only make the stock obsolete.

A French teacher signed up for French language magazines for the year for his whole set of 20 pupils, assuming that the parents would be willing to pay the extra £20 per term. They were not, so the academic department incurred an overspend of £1200.

A director of music purchased an organ for £200 from a local chapel that was being demolished. This was within his budget, but the final total cost included £50 delivery, £500 to have the asbestos that was discovered within it safely removed and £120 for the skip to scrap it in. It was never re-assembled and used as there was nowhere suitable to put it. Quite a bargain!

Disciplines

It is tempting to consider that a small overspend of a few hundred pounds does not really matter, particularly in the context of the high percentage of costs tied up in salaries and premises expenses. However, every little helps, and if overspends go unchecked, it sends out a message that the budget does not need to be taken seriously. There should, of course be an acceptable route for requests for extra funds to be considered, as unexpected items do occur, but this emphasis on *approval prior to expenditure* is an important boundary to establish.

Setting the budget

This is a long process that probably needs to be started soon after Christmas. If your school gives a one term notice of fee increases, the whole budget will need to be approved by the governors at least in outline by Easter. By then, you will only just have finalised the results of the first term of the current year. A crystal ball may be useful at this point. Early discussions with the Head and/or admissions officer concerning pupil numbers will probably be strained, as they will say that it is much too soon to know – which, of course, it is. Nevertheless, numbers must somehow be agreed for inclusion in draft one of the budget.

Another key budget discussion point is the level of bursaries/scholarships to allow for. With the recent heightened awareness of the need to fulfil public benefit requirements, many schools are seeking gradually to increase the means tested element of their allowances.

It has also been indicated that there should be some provision of full or virtually full bursaries, although the minimum acceptable level is not clear. Of course, bursaries are a worthy cause for due consideration anyway, even if they had not been thrust quite so forcibly on to our agenda by the Charity Commission.

Each year, the costs budget should be prepared from scratch, with items fully assessed and justified. Simply adding on a bit to last year's figures is not acceptable. It is good practice to involve heads of departments as much as is practicable, as this should result in a greater commitment to keep within the final budgets as set.

You will need input from the Head or deputy head concerning the academic departments, too, because you will not necessarily know which subjects have a change of set text or revised syllabus to deal with – or other possible changes and developments of which the heads of department (HoD) may not yet be aware. Always give feedback to the HoD. If a specific request has *not* been approved, it is useful to explain the reason – is there no chance ever, or is it worth trying again the following year?

Controls

If tight budgetary control is to succeed, there must be full support from the Head, so it is important to liaise closely, in order to ensure that you can present a united front on most, if not all, aspects of the budget. This will be particularly important when the draft budget is presented to the finance committee. It is best, if possible, to go through the main budget assumptions with the chairman of finance beforehand, so that any particular queries s/he raises can be researched and considered before the meeting.

Scrutiny and approval

The level of detail to present at the finance meeting will vary according to the requirements of your governors, but should always include a summary of the major issues and assumptions. These include:

- Pupil numbers with explanation for any major changes from the previous year.
- Proposed fee increases for each category of pupil.
- Salary increase proposals.
- Rate used for general inflation.
- Any structural changes.
- A final summary showing how the proposals fit into the longer range development plans.

A simple summary of the budget figures as compared with the previous year's actual results, together with the forecast for the current year, will help to show how reasonable your proposals are.

Reporting and monitoring

At last the new academic year starts, and reality can begin to be compared with your budget, which was agreed up to six months before. Some things, small and/or large, will have changed, but the budget should not usually need to be amended. Instead, variances from budget should be fully explained, and the expected result for the year re-forecast.

The first step is monitoring revenue and expenditure throughout the term. Budget holders should know how to check expenditure to date, and the bursar needs to get reports of serious over-spends as soon as possible: finding out at the end of term is too late.

Again, the effective tackling of any offenders relies on the Head and bursar showing a united front. For most schools the bulk of the income arrives at the start of each term, and is then gradually spent on salaries and utilities in a reasonably predictable pattern. I therefore believe that termly management accounts supplemented by monthly cash flow reports give a suitable reporting format.

The internal management accounts can be as detailed as you like, but do consider how much detail it is useful to distribute to the governors, bearing in mind how many other reports there will be in their meeting packs. Again, a pre-meeting with the chairman of finance is useful before the papers go out, to identify any items requiring special explanation and to clarify what governors would like to see included in the pack.

It is best to be able to avoid duplication of discussions at the finance meeting and governing board, so the details from the former meeting should be summarised with an overall executive summary for the latter. The key figures can usually be extracted and tabulated on to a couple of sheets of paper, to give a good overview. It is not helpful to adopt the tactics of one old lag bursar, which were to produce very detailed sheets in a very small font size to discourage questions.

Always communicate

It is your job to make the financial information accessible, so that the Head and governors can understand the financial results of the school. Nobody likes unpleasant surprises, so if an unexpected and expensive item needs funding, flag it up at once: do not wait until the end of term accounts. Present the bad news with your full report: comparative quotes for the new roof, or an explanation of the lost summer school booking *etc*.

This is another situation where the support of the Head is essential – so if possible, set up a system of regular feedback, sharing good, as well as bad, news. The team approach is ideal, but if the Head prefers to work as a 'lone wolf' s/he will probably never change. Better therefore to find a way to provide him/her with the relevant information as effectively as you can.

Reporting key indices for the results is useful in identifying trends over time; it also allows comparisons with industry benchmarking reports. Participation in one of these benchmarking exercises is a good way to give the governors a perspective for assessing your results, without risking trouble with the Office of Fair Trading.

Cash flow reports

Cash is the life-blood of any business, and must be effectively managed. The pattern of termly income covering regular monthly expenses means that many schools start each term in credit and end in overdraft, until the next term's fees arrive. Banks are very particular these days about reviewing overdraft facilities, and you will need to satisfy their requirements in order to keep the overdraft facility available at the appropriate level, and the rate of interest to the minimum possible.

The bank will wish to see your cash flow projections, and will monitor how well you keep to them. If an unexpected cash requirement arises, seek immediate approval from the bank: unauthorised exceeding of the overdraft limit could mean that the facility is withdrawn. On a happier note, if your school is well-funded, you will need to forecast the cash flow accurately so that funds can be invested to optimise interest receivable.

Statutory accounts

If the school is set up as a limited company and/or registered charity, the management accounts get audited at the end of the year and converted into the statutory accounts for filing with the Charity Commission and/or Companies House. This quite lengthy document is not a particularly popular read for the governors, but does have a certain importance, as it is a published document available for anyone to view.

It is an opportunity to hold forth about the ethos of the school and also to publicise the public benefit that the school seeks to provide, as well as reporting the historic results. I have never heard of a parent or prospective parent raising a query about an item in the statutory accounts, but accuracy is still important, and the audit gives external comfort to all interested parties that there is nothing untoward in the way that the school finances are managed.

The strategic plan

The strategic, or development, plan has traditionally been a much maligned document described by one bursar as: 'A complete waste of time and effort, which is out of date as soon as completed and too unwieldy to be of use.' However, the principle of looking up from day-to-day operations to plan for the future is necessary for any successful business, and most schools are now essentially businesses with an educational focus.

The core business is obviously the school, or schools, but there could also be a fundraising foundation; a trading company running lettings and sports centre activities; an Old Boys'/Girls' society; a Friends of the School association *etc*. *Not* to harness this wealth of available support resources is a waste. After all, most people involved only want to help the school, and there should be a way to channel this energy effectively.

Unless the relationships are nurtured carefully and continuously, these different elements of the school will operate as a collection of disparate small businesses, based on the same site. They will not necessarily have the same aspirations as the school management unless they are included in the information loop and given the chance to have a say.

They will be quick to pick up hints that the Head and/or bursar view their input as trivial or rather irritating, so make every reasonable effort to pull together the whole network into a cohesive organisation aiming to achieve optimum results. It may take some time and effort to get there, however: we have all heard of tales such as the Friends Society that was not very friendly, or the Old Boys'/Girls' Society that would only release funds for a 'modern sculpture' rather than the IT upgrade requested by the school.

The planning for major projects is discussed elsewhere in this book, so suffice it to say here that they need to be factored into the overall strategic plan. This could be where there is danger of some friction. If various ambitious scenarios are met with a negative response from the bursar, it could lead to the Head advancing his next pet project directly to the governors, to the complete surprise of the bursar. This does not leave the governors with confidence in the executive team. So, a collaborative approach is most productive, with realistic assessment of all suggestions.

Define your priorities

Find a way to agree how the top priorities can be achieved, even if a long timescale seems to be the only way. As bursar you will not wish to be just a recorder of details, but to have a real input to the business strategy. The financial section of the strategic plan needs to include cash flow forecasts for each year, to show the combined effects of the operating results and capital projects upon the bank balance.

As for the format of the document, there is no doubt that some plans are too long and, as a result, rarely referred to. If your plan is to be at all useful, it should have a clear summary that highlights major areas of focus for the next year, together with larger projects with a longer term development plan. Most plans look ahead for at least three years, but each school will decide the period most suitable for them. Once formulated, the plan should then be reviewed and updated each year, as the final step in the financial cycle.

Keep things under regular review

And finally... It has been difficult to write about financial management without being rather prescriptive, with many 'should' and 'must' statements, but that is the nature of the topic. Certain controls and procedures *must* be in place, but the style of implementing the procedures and communicating the results can make a very significant difference. If the Head and governors do not have a clear view of the school finances, you need to revise the reporting methods or formats. Effective control of the finances relies on the Head and bursar working together and supporting each other in public, even if individual items are hotly debated in private.

Good financial control may be taken for granted, but if it is lacking, the consequences will not take long to appear, and may take much longer to correct. Controlling and accurately reporting the results are only the first steps: using this information to enlarge and develop the business is the essential and interesting next stage. At its best, financial management brings the business to life.

The role of bursar is fascinating and varied, often undertaken in a very attractive setting. The finances are only part of that role, but they bring together all aspects of the business, providing invaluable information upon which to assess current operations and future plans.

Chapter 7

Buildings and maintenance

Richard Metcalfe

In a recent job description for a bursar's post the first item on the list of responsibilities was finance, which had 14 sub-sections. The next two items, staffing matters and premises, had one line each. While it is neither uncommon nor surprising to see financial matters at the top of the list, premises are a rather more significant and complex matter than a single line would suggest: it is worth pausing to remember that, while money doesn't kill people (at least, not directly), electricity, gas, water and fire – for which the premises staff are responsible – sadly can, and do, cause fatalities. We should also never lose sight of the fact that the responsibilities associated with managing premises and building matters are enforced by criminal, as well as civil, law.

Those same responsibilities should not, therefore, be underestimated. Quite apart from these safety issues, premises play a crucial role in setting the image of the school: if parents on their first visit approach via a pot-holed drive or a reception area with peeling paint, they will form a first and lasting impression that may not do justice to all other aspects of the school. Parents are also likely to expect warm, airy and well-lit classrooms, with all the latest technology in evidence.

So, where do you start with buildings? While the process is never-ending, there seems to be some logic in looking first at a significant refurbishment or building project, then at how premises are maintained, and finally to note some other bits and pieces that go along with them.

Project management

The starting point for a building project is to define what you seek within the school's overall development plan and, rather than identify one solution, form a clear statement of objectives that has the backing of all the key stakeholders, including whoever is going to provide the funding. Leave it to the design team to come up with the solutions, as a fresh pair of eyes will often come up with a far better proposal: often one that the school has never even considered or thought possible.

You also need a solution that will allow some flexibility over timings, and make it possible to keep future options open. One of the few certainties is that needs are bound to change during the lifetime of the building. You should not underestimate the design requirements if the building is to be open to the public, and you must be aware of the preferential VAT arrangements that can be achieved through certain aspects of the building and its design.

However, you still need to look closely at proposals to check that they will work in practice. Are the corridors wide enough for several hundred students tramping in both directions every time the bell rings? Are they maintainable (for example, how are you supposed to clean the glass roof of that atrium safely)? Can they be constructed without bringing the routine life of the school to a complete halt, through necessary access for contractors, noisy activities during exam periods, *etc*?

You should also make sure that you are happy about compliance with statutory requirements such as the fire regulations and the Disability Discrimination Act (DDA), and about what the building's energy consumption and carbon footprint will be. In summary, you must satisfy yourself about the entire life cost of the building.

Other statutory compliance issues include the Building Regulations (overseen either by the local council's building control section or by a consultant appointed by the school) and the Construction, Design and Management (CDM) Regulations (overseen by the Health and Safety Executive: HSE), which place criminal responsibilities on the school acting as client, as well as on the design team and contractor.

There are two important points in managing the costs of a project that require the bursar to keep a close eye on all estimates. First, the construction industry almost without exception will quote costs exclusive of VAT. So this needs to be added to all net costs, as in the vast majority of cases the school will not be able to recover the VAT on non-residential buildings. There are ways of reducing the VAT liability on new development in particular circumstances, but specialist advice should be taken if these are to be considered.

Secondly, the design team is unlikely to consider costs outside the contract, the most significant of which is likely to be furniture and equipment purchased directly by the school. However, these costs may also include planning fees, and insurance and removal costs. All these add-ons need to be included in the master cost plan, which the bursar is well-advised to maintain and use as a basis for reporting to governors and funders.

The project team

The conventional approach to a building project is to appoint first an architect, then the other members of the design team; next to go through various iterations of design and costing and then to invite tenders from contractors, which should be carefully examined with the design team that will eventually supervise the construction contract.

In appointing architects, it is very important to remember that they will often have two important roles, depending on the extent of their mandate and the stages of RIBA-recommended work that they undertake. These are likely to include the design and specification for the work and (something often overlooked) the supervision of the contract – although it should also be said that the architect does not *necessarily* also have to be the one who carries out this role.

It is also vital to employ an architect who will listen to, understand and articulate your requirements, and who will provide what the school actually requires rather than what they, the architects, think it ought to have. The RIBA publishes guidelines on services provided and rates of fees – the latter to be regarded as a basis for negotiation rather than fixed rate.

The remainder of the design team may include one or more of the following:

- a quantity surveyor (usually Royal Institution of Chartered Surveyors, RICS), who is responsible for detailed aspects of estimating and cost control;
- a structural engineer (Institute of Civil Engineers, ICE), dealing with the things that will make sure that the building stands up;

- a services engineer (Association of Consulting Engineers, ACE), dealing with the mechanical (heating, ventilation, plumbing, *etc*), electrical and other service installations.

Depending on the nature of the project you may need other specialists, often including a landscape architect (Landscape Institute) and possibly an acoustics consultant (Institute of Acoustics). Other specialists include theatre and sports consultants. There may be some small projects where, rather than an architect, a building surveyor (also RICS) will be appropriate.

Larger projects may warrant a separate projects manager, in which case, his/her role, responsibilities and lines of communication should be absolutely clear, and any sizeable project should have a clerk of works, traditionally appointed by (and sometimes an employee of) the client, who acts as the eyes and ears on site for the client and design team, inspecting the work and keeping records of activity on site.

Co-ordination and communication

The architect will normally be the lead consultant, acting as contract administrator; providing minutes of meetings; distributing drawings and documents and contract documents. One absolutely critical point is to be clear as to who is responsible for the co-ordination of the design. If this is not done properly, you risk having electrical sockets behind radiators and steelwork across windows (yes it can, and does, happen!). Early planning of ICT and furniture needs is essential in this context.

The lines of communication between this team and the school (not to mention those *within* the school!) need to be clearly defined. Ideally there should be one point of contact for the school (step forward the bursar or the facilities manager!) and one for the design team (normally the architect). To avoid confusion, wasted effort, time and money, all communications between the school and the design team (and, later, the contractor) should be conducted through those two people. The bursar or designated colleague must be seen as a partner in the design and construction process – 'partnership' being very much the buzz-word in the construction industry. S/he might even come to enjoy regular meetings with 16 people cramped round a table in a Portakabin...

Planning consent

At an early stage in the design, it is important to involve the local planning authority. This is not only because the proposal has to be consistent with local planning policies and criteria, but also because you need to carry the planners with you. This will almost inevitably include an element of give and take, and/or occasionally humouring some whim of a particular planner, but either way it will increase the likelihood of securing planning consent.

If your site is in a conservation area and your buildings are listed and/or of historic significance, the planning and consultation process will be more onerous and will involve other bodies such as English Heritage. Any sizeable contract is now likely to attract a need for additional planning documentation such as a Travel Plan, BREAM assessment or Environmental Impact Assessment – and may include other requirements such as tree protection or improving the local access road under what is known as a Section 106 Agreement. Processing of an application will take at least eight, and possibly as many as 16, weeks or even more, depending on size, location, complexity and the local response to the project.

It is also well worth involving the school's neighbours in some form of consultative process during this stage. Not only is it good PR, but it tends also to be a winner with the planning authorities.

Tendering and contractors

Once you have an agreed design and specification, together with a realistic and acceptable estimate of cost and certainty of securing planning consent by a given date, the next stage is to invite tenders for the work. The nature and extent of the tender documents will vary according to the size and complexity of the project, from a few drawings and short specification to a massive set of drawings and specifications with a full bill of quantities (a large, detailed document drawn up by the quantity surveyor).

Depending on the size of the project a tender list might typically include four to six contractors who have been contacted by the design team, and who have been identified as both competent and available to carry out the work. The temptation to invite a long list of contractors to tender is to be avoided. Whatever some small contractors claim, there is no such thing as a 'free estimate': tendering is an expensive process for contractors and they are more likely to give a keen price if they know they are one of a small number competing for the work on a level playing field.

You also need a contractor who has an understanding of the special issues relating to working in a school. A company will cause you huge problems if it thinks that it does not matter if the job overruns to October; that it can drill at will into the walls of the sports hall during exams; or employ operatives only able to work accompanied by the output of a large ghetto-blaster and still inclined to comment loudly on the physical characteristics of passing young females.

I have always favoured this 'conventional' procurement route, but it is by no means the only way of running a project. The most common other means is Design and Build. The difference can probably most simply be described by saying that in the conventional route the client's team specify the 'outputs' for the project, whereas for design and build they specify the 'inputs' and the contractor determines most 'outputs'.

A typical route for Design and Build would be to pay an architect to produce a scheme that can secure planning consent, and then invite contractors to tender for the detailed design and construction of the building. While there is a valid argument that contractors know more about constructing buildings than architects, most contactors lack the in-house expertise to complete the exercise themselves and will employ consultants to carry out the work, sometimes 'novating' the original architect to work for them.

Design and Build is often regarded as a safe route for fairly basic buildings (such as a small block of classrooms), but it is absolutely essential to get the original specification of requirements correct in all detail, in particular for a more complex project. A school would be well-advised to appoint a project manager to act for them under such a project.

Building contracts

There exists a plethora of other procurement routes and contracts, some highly complex. For example, two-stage tendering with a maximum guaranteed price might well be appropriate for a large and complex or phased project. There is also an increasing element of contractor-designed components in otherwise 'traditional' contracts. Whichever route is used, it is strongly recommended that an industry standard form contract is used, those provided by the Joint Contracts Tribunal (JCT) being the most common.

A particular aspect of contracts that is commonly misunderstood is 'penalties'. A Head or governor may often suggest that the contract should include a penalty clause to keep the contractor on his toes. In fact, most standard contracts include provision for 'liquidated and ascertained damages', *ie* genuine costs to the client arising from a delay or some other problem for which the contractor is responsible, at a pre-determined rate stated in the contract. Adding 'penalties' to a standard contract is very likely merely to increase the tender price and the potential for disputes.

Building maintenance

So, once you have your building, how do you go about maintaining it? For a start, do not make the mistake of assuming that a new building does not require any ongoing care. The service installations in most new buildings are far more complex than in the past and they require regular maintenance – for example, Building Energy Management Systems (BEMS); addressable fire detection systems and the automatic doors and lifts necessary for DDA compliance.

However, your approach to maintenance obviously has to cover the whole estate, and this needs some kind of structure. The question is best addressed by making the shift from purely reactive maintenance (*ie* only fixing things as and after they fail) to preventative and pre-planned maintenance, and there is a range of software packages available to support this process. However, this approach comes at a price, and a small school may find it an expensive luxury.

The structure can be provided by means of a maintenance strategy based on a survey of the whole estate (including external elements such as roadways, street lighting and drains). This is usually known as a condition survey, carried out by a team of building and engineering professionals. The exercise will grade each element of each building (*eg* roof, windows, electrical distribution and boilers) according to its condition and life expectancy. A grading structure might be on the lines of:

1. Serious risk of failure.
2. Major repair/replacement required as a priority.
3. Operational but requires repair/replacement during an identified period.
4. Operational and requires only routine repair/replacement.

From these gradings it is possible to prioritise maintenance work. Typically, this might look at a ten-year period, with specific elements scheduled for each of the next five years according to priority, and less urgent work included as a block in years six to ten, to be allocated to a specific year later as the programme rolls on. Estimates of cost are then attached to each element of work so that a fully costed programme for the next five to ten years can be established and fed into the whole school budgeting process.

In providing costs for such a relatively long period it is important to be clear on the cost base used: using the costs from an established index current at the time of the survey is safer than guessing inflation in the building trades over the next ten years – and don't forget professional fees, VAT and some contingency.

The planned maintenance schedule also needs to include all the regular contracts for servicing engineering installations, and for regular statutory requirements such as Portable Appliance Testing (PAT) and legionella testing. Furthermore, it should make provision for dealing with hazardous materials, not least asbestos, for which there is a legal requirement to have a register of known materials in the school's property.

Even the most thorough pre-planned maintenance arrangements cannot, of course, eliminate the need for some reactive maintenance: windows will be broken; a roof will leak at that particularly inaccessible point and a heating pump will simply give up the ghost one winter morning. It is therefore important to include an allowance for such reactive work and have the resources to respond to it.

Managing maintenance

Who should do this work? Large facilities management (FM) companies will tell you that only a fool of a Head would have his own staff doing this work and that all aspects of property management should be outsourced in a 'Total FM' solution, leaving the bursar and Head free to concentrate on the school's core activities. This approach is now common in large PFI projects, including hospitals and academies.

Most bursars will tell you that you cannot underestimate the value of your own maintenance man, with his intimate knowledge of every heating valve and inspection cover – though it is very important that the bursar or facilities manager knows just what it is safe and legal for school staff to touch. This applies particularly to work on gas and electrical installations, which must be carried out by operatives certified as competent to deal with them.

The best solution lies somewhere between these two extremes: having good guys on site and knowing when to call in the experts, and whom to call. While the large FM companies will have the expertise, they will lack the local knowledge and some may not have a full understanding of the issues of working in a school, which nowadays must include pupil safeguarding considerations as well as normal customer care issues. It is also important to remember that many maintenance problems arise during silent hours, so that there must be adequate and cost effective arrangements in place to provide 24/7 cover for key services.

Most schools are likely at present to retain a range of specialist contractors such as electricians, heating engineers and alarm companies. In retaining such contractors it is good to strike a balance between having a contractor with a good working knowledge of the site, but also market testing his services from time to time to make sure that the charges reflect the state of the market.

This might be done by obtaining tenders for a term contract in which the contractor gives a firm price for the routine annual servicing element for one or more years; a price for the known pre-planned work, and a schedule of rates for any unscheduled or reactive work that may be required during the contract period. This will give the bursar and the school a greater degree of cost certainty when setting up the school budget.

Some other aspects of premises management

What other aspects of property management are there to exercise the minds of school management? In recent times increasing attention has been paid to the importance of conserving energy, managing waste and reducing inefficiencies. This calls on a wide range of new and developing technologies such as LED lights, heat source pumps, and recycling.

I have not touched on what are now termed 'soft' facilities management aspects such as caretaking and cleaning, but it is important never to forget that they are highly visible to users of the school. Meanwhile there remain a number of aspects of which most teaching staff – and many governors – will be unaware. These include unfathomable leases; the utter fascination of drainage easements; the dark art of rateable values; the apparent randomness of water and drainage charges and all aspects of insurance.

Other responsibilities include liaison with local authorities on a range of planning and local amenity issues; with the fire service and the Health and Safety Executive; and with specialist consultants and contractors in dealing with matters such as asbestos removal – all the while keeping abreast of developments in technology and markets. Last, and certainly not least, safeguarding requirements make it essential for the school to ensure that all those who come to work on its site do so without presenting any kind of risk to the pupils and staff in the school.

Who does all this?

Who should manage all this? In a small prep school the bursar will recognise his/her contribution to all aspects, whether with drain rods in hand or sitting round the table at the finance committee explaining project and maintenance costs. Most large schools now have someone in the role of estates bursar, often known as facilities manager in modern parlance.

There is also an increasing range of routes for staff to gain qualifications in this area through organisations such as Asset Skills and the British Institute of Facilities Management, as well as degree courses in FM at universities such as Sheffield Hallam.

Whoever finds themselves with these responsibilities will certainly not have a dull life, nor wonder how to entertain themselves through the school holidays – and hopefully they should also find themselves making a genuine contribution to the success of a school by the value added through well-designed, constructed and maintained facilities.

Chapter 8

Large-scale strategic planning and project management

Alison Shakespeare

For most bursars, large-scale projects do not come along very often. Every project is different – be it major building work, merging two schools, changing the age range at the school, going coeducational, or phasing out boarding in favour of more day pupils. What large scale strategic projects are likely to have in common, however, is the significant commitment of time and resources over a period of months or even years, and implications for most, if not all, staff within the bursary. The day job of running the school continues, while simultaneously a major project is added into the mix.

I am writing primarily from my experience of building a new school on a 75-acre green field site and relocating two coeducational day schools. At the date of the move, Leicester Grammar Junior School and Leicester Grammar School had 995 pupils, aged three to 18, on separate sites several miles apart. The £35m relocation project brought the two schools together for the first time, with state-of-the-art facilities.

Bringing two schools together on a new site had far-reaching implications for the day-to-day running of the schools. New staff had to be recruited, including a whole team of grounds staff, which had not been required at the old city-centre sites, which lacked green space. The catering team was expanded and menus were reviewed. New bus routes were established, operated directly by the school for the first time, which involved transporting more than 400 pupils per day during the first term.

Everything had to be reconsidered, from the timing of the school day to the procedure to be followed in the event of a fire drill. The Trust required a significant increase in pupil numbers to fill the new larger buildings and to fund the new facilities. This required a concerted marketing strategy and, at the time of writing, the school roll has risen by 20% in just three years (despite our move taking place during a recession).

This chapter considers some of the lessons that can be learned from a major strategic project, and explores some of the themes that are likely to be common to other projects.

From vision to action: getting started

The decision to embark on a major strategic project is very unlikely to be taken by the bursar alone. Such projects are, by definition, about the strategic direction of the whole school and are likely to evolve following a period of discussion between the trustees/governors and the senior management team.

It is essential that the trustees and the senior management team have a clear, shared, vision when embarking on the project. Once the project is underway, there is no room for doubts as to whether you should be undertaking it: the focus must turn to *how* to achieve your objectives. If you do not have a clear vision of what you want to achieve, you will find it increasingly difficult to provide direction to staff and consultants, or to persuade pupils and parents of the benefits to come in the future.

Once the initial decisions have been taken, do not underestimate how long it may take to get a major project underway. Taking as an example major building work, the site needs to be identified; plans drawn up; discussions held with heritage bodies and ecologists; and planning permission obtained. Budgets must be set; tender documents sent out and contractors identified. Approval for major decisions will be required from a board of trustees that may ordinarily meet only three or four times a year. While steps can, and should, be taken to avoid unnecessary delays, it is important to be realistic at the point of project embarkation.

Limiting factors

In any project there will be key limiting factors and it is essential that these are identified and understood at the outset. Does the project have to be completed by a particular date? Is the budget particularly tight? Are you carrying out building work within the main school site during term-time, close to occupied teaching blocks and boarding houses? Identify the key limiting factor that may constrain future decisions and ensure that everyone recognises the importance of this overriding consideration.

By the time the builders actually entered the site to build the new Grammar School, the key limiting factor was time. The process of obtaining planning permission to build on the site was lengthy and involved a public inquiry. The schools were determined to open at the new site at the start of an academic year, and the builders confirmed that, although timescales were challenging, they could complete by 1st September 2008.

The decision was taken to relocate both schools in time for the start of that term. Everyone was made aware of the importance of completing the work on time and any subsequent discussion of a possible variation to the scope of works included the question: would this change have any impact upon the completion date?

With unlimited time and money, most things are possible! Understand and manage the constraints within which you are operating.

Teamwork

A major project is a team effort and it is essential that there are clear lines of reporting and clear areas of responsibility. This is particularly important where more than one senior member of staff is heading up the project – perhaps the bursar and the Head, or the finance bursar and the estates bursar. There will be a lot of work that does not fall neatly into anyone's job description and you cannot afford to waste time duplicating effort in some areas and missing other things completely.

The project may well involve most of the staff who report to you, in one way or another. Involve them at as early a stage as possible, so they have the maximum amount of time to carry out the work you are passing on to them. Remember that they too are juggling their normal workload alongside the project.

Delegate according to the skills and abilities of your staff. Some people work well under pressure and are good at problem-solving. Others work best when they have a defined task to complete within a less frenetic timescale. You will know what is within the capabilities of your staff, and how much direction they will need in order to complete a task.

The success of a project depends in no small measure on the quality of the teamwork. A disparate group of staff, contractors and consultants will be carrying out work that does not form part of the school's day-to-day routine. These individuals need to work together towards a common goal, sure of their role and responsibilities within the project as a whole.

The use of consultants

There is no hard and fast rule governing which work should be carried out by consultants, rather than by staff employed directly by the school.

Key factors to consider include whether your staff are properly qualified and experienced to complete a task, and whether they have enough time available. In some instances particular equipment or computer software might be required, making it more cost-effective to bring in a specialist. Sometimes you may want the comfort of knowing that someone else's professional indemnity insurance can be called upon in the event of problems!

If a task requires a high degree of knowledge of how your individual school operates, it may be more effective (and cheaper) for a member of staff to do the work. If a task is best carried out by someone with experience of similar projects, you may choose to bring in a consultant.

One area where Leicester Grammar School chose to bring in a consultant was to manage the removals process. The schools occupied six separate buildings before moving to Great Glen. A consultant was used to oversee the logistics of the removals process, working closely with staff and with the removal firm, over a period of several months.

The school benefited enormously from his experience of similar large-scale removals, and his ability to foresee possible problems before they arose. Co-ordinating the removal process was a full-time job for several weeks, at a key point in the project, and it is my belief that no member of staff could have set aside the amount of time that was required to carry out this task effectively.

Appointing a consultant

A consultant is someone who is not employed directly by the school, but who is contracted to carry out work for the school. It is essential that a written contract is in place, which specifies the work to be undertaken, and the cost, whether quoted as a fixed price or an hourly rate. Do not rely on verbal agreements, and do not assume that consultants somehow know what you want them to do without your needing to tell them. There should be a clear scope of work, agreed outcomes and regular reporting.

When appointing a consultant, you will usually be buying in relevant skills and depth of experience – not just ‘another pair of hands’ – so ensure that you are drawing on their core competencies. It is for you to decide whether their expertise needs to have been gained carrying out similar work for other independent schools. Sometimes work carried out for other types of organisation may be just as relevant.

Consider how much face-to-face contact will be required with the consultant during the project. Does the work need to be completed at school, or at the consultant’s own office? How frequently will you require the consultant to visit the school?

If you require a high degree of face-to-face contact, it may mean appointing a consultant who is based geographically close to the school. If consultants are based a significant distance away, how will they ensure that they are available on site when required? How much will you be required to pay in travel time and mileage if they do come to site? If you require frequent meetings that involve a 300-mile round trip, the cost to the school could rise considerably and it is likely to be more difficult to arrange meetings if 30 minutes of meeting time fills up half a day of the consultant’s time.

Availability of key individuals is also an issue to consider. Large consultancy companies would ordinarily be expected to provide an ongoing service during holiday periods, by substituting other staff to cover for absent colleagues. However, smaller companies and sole traders are likely to find this more difficult. If you require the work to be carried out during a particular period (for instance during July and August), establish at the outset that the consultant will be available to work during the critical period and can commit to meeting your deadlines.

If the work will be carried out primarily by one person, ensure that you meet that person and not just the sales team: personalities matter, and you need to appoint someone with whom you can work, and who understands your requirements. My advice is to seek a consultant who listens before offering advice. No two projects are identical and no two schools are identical. A consultant who thinks you are the same as a previous client is likely to misinterpret your requirements. A consultant who listens and gains an understanding of the project and the school's aims is far more likely to work *with* you and to provide relevant advice that helps you achieve your goals.

There is rarely, if ever, only one company that can do the job. Seek competitive quotes and consider the options. Always take up references before confirming an appointment.

Managing a consultant

A consultant is working for you, and is part of the team that is delivering the project. Put time aside for regular meetings, to ensure that consultants are sticking to their brief. Ensure that they are aware of relevant deadlines that may arise as a result of work carried out by others.

Ensure you are sufficiently familiar with the consultant's contract that you know what the consultant should be doing. And beware of asking the consultant to stray outside that brief: it will almost certainly have cost implications, and it may determine whether or not the core work is completed on time. If you are making changes, ask for confirmation of whether (i) cost or (ii) completion date will be affected.

Communication

A large-scale project is likely to affect most of your staff and pupils directly and to be of interest to a wider group of stakeholders. This adds up to a sizeable number of people who want/need to know what is happening and what will happen next. The best way to prevent rumours from taking hold is to provide accurate, reliable information.

The mechanics of communicating with staff are relatively straightforward – you will see most of them each day, and will have the ability to send out regular emails. My advice is to err on the side of caution and tell staff more than you think they really need to know. Some people deal with change extremely well. Others will feel anxious about changes that you may consider to be relatively minor. On the whole, people feel less anxious when they have more information. Remember that many staff are likely to be involved in the project in some way, so the information you are sending out will also assist them in carrying out their work.

Highlight the positive outcomes of the forthcoming changes (a bigger office; better IT; new classroom furniture); but also acknowledge aspects of the project that may be less appealing (budget reductions; a requirement to come in to school to unpack boxes during the summer holidays; an enforced change in working hours). Staff must be able to trust the information they are receiving and be confident that you are revealing the full picture.

When communicating with parents and the local community, thought should be given to what information they need to receive and how to disseminate it. The school website is likely to be a good medium for issuing regular updates. Remember that current and future parents pay your salary and keep the school solvent, and you need to explain to them what changes you are making and how those changes will improve the education you offer to their children.

Towards the end of the project

However well you plan, something is bound to go wrong, so my advice is to prepare for the unexpected and be ready to think on your feet! The things that go wrong are likely to be those that you were so sure would go smoothly that you didn't worry about them at all. Unfortunately I have no tips for reliably spotting these pitfalls in advance, and can only suggest doing your best and preparing yourself psychologically for a busy period in the latter stages of the project.

The unexpected problem I faced when the Grammar School moved was the catering staff's lack of experience of serving lunch to younger children. The catering staff had come from the old senior school site and were therefore used to pupils aged ten to 18. On the first day of term, they were faced with some 350 junior school pupils aged from three to ten. The staff were their usual friendly selves, asking the children what they would like to eat. Unfortunately, it takes rather a long time for a three year-old to decide and time ticked by as the children slowly made their way through the servery, being given a choice of main course, vegetable, potato, drink and dessert.

The new building has one kitchen and servery, and the senior school pupils eat after the junior school. On the first day of term, it took so long to serve lunch to the junior school that some unfortunate seniors were still having their lunch at 3.30pm when the younger children were going home! The catering staff speeded up considerably on the second day of term.

Do not underestimate how long it will take to return to 'normality' after a major project. There will be ongoing snagging following the handover of a new building. There will be staff who ask endless questions as they move into the new building. There will be things you didn't quite get right, or people who change their mind late in the day about what they wanted. And then, at some point several months after you had expected the project to 'finish', you will realise that you are, once again, spending most of your time running the school.

In conclusion

Have a clear vision of what you want to achieve, and think through the implications of the changes you are making. Be realistic about how much work you personally can fit into a day. Delegate, and bring in consultants accordingly, to ensure that deadlines are met. Do not be afraid to seek advice: no one can claim to be an expert in everything and if someone else has already grappled with the issues you face, why re-invent the wheel?

Remember to make use of the bursar network and the ISBA. During the project I have described here, I frequently drew on the experience of bursars at other schools. When faced with the task of recruiting and equipping a team of grounds staff from scratch (and without any direct experience to draw on, as I had not previously worked at a school) I turned to other bursars and arranged meetings with head groundsmen at other schools, in order better to understand their work.

And finally, *communicate* as much, and as often, as possible. The success of a large project depends ultimately on the quality of the teamwork, and the task of bringing that team together is at the heart of your role.

Chapter 9

Clerk to the governors

Roy Blackwell

It probably goes without saying that no two schools are the same, and that this is a dictum that applies as much to the question of whether one person should combine the roles of bursar and clerk (and to precisely how the clerk carries out the role), as to any other aspect of a school's *modus operandi*. Nevertheless, I offer the following, based on my own experience, and starting with a job description.

The job description

1. The clerk to the governing body will be accountable to the governing body, working effectively with the chair of governors and with the Head and other governors. The clerk will be responsible for advising the governing body on constitutional matters, duties and powers and will work within the broad current legislative framework. S/he will secure the continuity of governing body business and observe confidentiality requirements.
2. Meetings. The clerk to the governing body will:
   - work effectively with the chair and Head before the governing body meeting to prepare an agenda that takes account of the legislative framework, priorities identified by the school and any standing items;
   - encourage the Head and members of the governing body to produce agenda papers on time;
   - produce, collate and distribute the agenda and papers so that recipients receive them at least seven, and preferably ten, clear days before the meeting;
   - record the attendance of governors at the meeting and take appropriate action where necessary;
   - advise the governing body on sound governance legislation and

procedural matters where necessary before, during and after the meeting;
- take notes of the governing body meetings to prepare minutes, including indicating who is responsible for any agreed action;
- record all decisions accurately and objectively with timescales for actions;
- send draft minutes within 15 school days (at the latest) to the chair and Head for amendment and approval;
- circulate the draft agenda to the chair and Head for approval well in advance of despatching the papers (ideally seven days before final despatch of the agenda papers);
- circulate the approved draft minutes along with the agenda for the next meeting to reach all governors at least seven full days before the next meeting; and
- act as chair for that part of the meeting at which the chair is elected.

3. Membership. The clerk will:

- maintain copies of current terms of reference and membership of committees and working parties and nominated liaison or special governors;
- advise governors and appointing bodies of the expiry of the term of office before the term expires so elections or appointments may be organised in a timely manner;
- inform the governing body of any changes to its membership;
- maintain governor meeting attendance records and advise the governing body of non-attendance of governors;
- annually have governors complete a declaration of business interests form and at each meeting declare any interests relating to that agenda; and
- check that criminal records bureau (CRB) disclosure has been successfully carried out on any governor when it is appropriate to do so.

4. Advice and information. The clerk will:

- advise the governing body on procedural issues;
- ensure that statutory policies are in place and that a file is kept in the

school of policies and other school documents approved by the governing body;
- have access to the appropriate legal advice;
- assist with the elections of governors as and when required;
- give advice and support to governors taking on new roles such as chair, vice chair or chair of a committee or new governor;
- participate in and contribute to the training of governors in areas appropriate to the clerking role;
- maintain a file of relevant documents;
- maintain archive materials; and
- (or may) clerk some or all statutory and non-statutory governing body committees, depending on how many meetings take place.

Putting flesh on the bones

The above describes the main functions/duties of the clerk, but it is important to understand the broader context in which you will operate. First, remember that you are at the governing body meeting in the role of clerk *and* as the bursar. At times, these roles may prove hard to reconcile. Consequently, you will need to give advice as clerk at times when, as bursar, you might prefer to remain silent.

If proper procedures are not being followed, or there is a potential conflict of interest in what is being discussed, you must bring this to the attention of the chair of governors. If someone starts to discuss a member of staff in detail at a meeting at which there are other staff present, you might need (or wish) to advise the chair either to have a general discussion about a personnel issue or to curtail the item altogether, temporarily, at least.

There may be meetings at which some governors try to pursue a personal agenda. For example, a governor who happens to be a parent should not use a meeting to bypass normal procedures (*ie* raise the matter at a governors' meeting before having seen the Head).

Likewise, governors may need reminding that governing body meetings are business meetings. They are more concerned with broad policy and are not conducive to very detailed discussion. Consequently, they need to be carefully planned, so your relationship with the chair is crucial in setting the tone, as well as the conduct, of the meeting before it starts.

Just as you will ensure papers are distributed *before* the meeting, so should others. The terms of reference for both the full board and its committees should lay down clear expectations in this respect: it is not good practice for governors to 'table' papers and, if they try to do so, you should aim to persuade the chair to defer detailed discussion on the paper until the next meeting. This will help to dissuade the tabling habit.

Likewise, try to persuade the chair to avoid allowing someone to read through a document s/he is presenting: governors should already have read it for themselves. It might be useful to offer templates for reports/papers, *etc*. For example, it might be helpful for every report to have clear recommendations at its conclusion.

Governors may also need reminding from time to time about conflict of interest statements, the confidentiality of governors' meetings and the need to abide by majority decisions.

Finally, the clerk is not just a minute taker. That job could, in fact, be delegated to someone else, both for the main governing body meeting and for its committees. It is the advisory role that is of the utmost importance, and governors need to feel they can trust you to keep them on the straight and narrow.

The Charity Commission, and its annual return

One of the areas where this is vitally important is in the audited accounts. Most independent schools are charities, either incorporated or unincorporated. As such, they must answer to the Charity Commission in terms of their conduct. They must also make an annual return to the Commission. As bursar, you would be involved in this exercise anyway, as this return includes the annual accounts. However, there is a great deal more to it than that, and the clerk to the governing body needs to ensure that governors are complying with *all* the Commission's requirements.

The annual return consists of several sections:

Part A – Charity information: this information forms part of the charity's entry on the register and includes contact and trustee details as well as income and expenditure.

Part B – Financial information: this contains detailed financial information about the charity from your annual accounts. The information given is displayed on the charity's register entry and shows the income, spending and assets of the charity.

Part C – Summary information return (SIR): The SIR provides an easily accessible summary of the charity's key achievements. This is displayed on the charity's entry on the Charity Commission register. It helps people understand what the charity does and how it has performed.

In addition to the annual return, you will need to submit to the Charity Commission the trustees' annual report (TAR) and accounts.

In preparing the TAR, the governing body has to agree their future objectives, and there has to be a review of past performance. Were objectives met? What are the priorities for the charity? What are its main aims? Governors need to agree on these.

The charity also needs to report any serious incidents. There is also a requirement to demonstrate public benefit in the return, and trustees/governors have to sign a declaration stating that they have complied with Section 4 of the Charities Act 2006, which deals with public benefit. There are a number of ways in which public benefit may be reported but, in essence, there needs to be a record of all the activities undertaken by the charity to further its charitable object and public benefit activities. Remember that this section will be looked at by the Commission when it is considering whether a charity is demonstrating public benefit.

All the information needs gathering and collating and the clerk is a key player in this exercise, as well as being one of the people to sign off the return when it is sent to the Charity Commission.

Incorporation

If you are an incorporated charity, you will also have to deal with Companies House. (Please note, this is in addition to the return to the Charity Commission.) There is no longer a particular category for audit exempt charitable companies in England and Wales, or in Scotland. They will qualify for audit exemption under company law in the same way as any other company. However, Northern Ireland charitable companies are still subject to the requirements of the 1988 Order to qualify for audit exemption and their accounts will need to reflect the relevant statements – which involves another annual return.

There are several sections involved. The annual return gives a snapshot of general information about a company's directors (normally, but not always, the governors); secretaries (clerk to the governing body); registered office address; shareholders and share capital if appropriate. The accounting reference date is the date that determines its financial year end. It is also the date that determines when accounts are due for delivery to Companies House.

All companies must prepare accounts for their members (governors) and for filing at Companies House. There is a deadline for delivering acceptable accounts which comply with all relevant legal requirements to Companies House. If you miss the deadline, Companies House will issue an automatic penalty, without exception. Companies House may also prosecute directors (normally governors) of a company for delivering their accounts late, or not at all.

Pros and cons of the bursar also being the clerk

The pros first: the demands described in the previous section, most of which involve information produced by the bursar as part of his/her responsibilities, support the argument for having the bursar also performing the role of clerk to the governing body.

Another obvious advantage of the bursar being the clerk is that s/he knows the school and is therefore well positioned to deal with many of the issues that fall to the clerk. In all normal circumstances s/he will be attending governing body meetings anyway. So, in reality, there will be a financial saving, especially when an alternative might be to pay for a minute-taker.

Additionally, as bursar you should also have ensured that you have up-to-date legal advice to carry out your normal bursarial functions. This will also help you to speak with authority about such matters in your role as clerk. It will also be important to agree the agenda in advance with chairman and the Head, and also to decide who will be dealing with, or leading on, particular items. Even in an age in which so much is decided via electronic methods, agenda planning meetings are still important. In practical/logistical terms it may be easier for the bursar to attend them than for an 'outside' clerk to come specially.

However, alongside these two advantages come some counter-arguments. The bursar needs to be ready and prepared to talk about and answer questions on any financial reports (or, indeed, any other items) on the agenda. You cannot guarantee that it will always be easy to be bursar and clerk at the same time, so you need to think ahead, aiming to anticipate any potential issues that might cause you to have conflicts of role. Likewise, the fact that the bursar is known to governors may lead some of them to think of him/her as a member of staff, rather than as someone giving impartial advice that they may not like.

The 'minute-taking argument' already stated can also be negated by the recognition that, as stated earlier, minute-taking is also the least of the duties of the clerk. Besides, the clerk does not necessarily have to take the minutes anyway: merely to be responsible for them.

There will be some issues that may lead to a conflict of interest if the bursar is also the clerk. There may be confidential items relating to a member of staff where it would not be appropriate for you to be in attendance – for example, if your presence might later be seen to prejudice any future appeal by a member of the support staff against dismissal. (A side-issue, but an important one, nevertheless: if any individual governors are likely to be involved in such an appeal, they should not be present when the governors discuss procedures ahead of the event; indeed, it could be argued that such a discussion should take place between individual governors informally, rather than in any such meeting.)

Remember, too, that appeal hearings do not merely involve you in taking notes at the hearing itself, but also in selecting a panel of governors; advising on procedures to be followed; and taking legal advice as to possible outcomes. With the ever-growing complexity of employment law and the litigious society in which we live, you cannot afford to be subject to challenge on the procedures used in such cases.

So, even if governors would like your involvement, they need to be reminded of the separate roles of bursar and clerk in such matters. There is, of course, always the option of employing a legal expert for occasions, but that can be expensive. All these eventualities could mean that someone else needs to perform the clerk's duties for a short time.

One other scenario needs also to be described. There have also been cases where a governor has tried to use the bursar to circumvent the Head. In such circumstances, being clerk to the governing body may lead some governors to believe that this makes such action legitimate – which could support the view that the two roles should be held by different people.

There is no unequivocally right answer. Whichever way the decision over bursar/clerk finally goes, one basic requirement needs to be emphasised: in all schools there need to be unambiguous contractual requirements and very clear lines of management and accountability. The chairman, Head and clerk/bursar need to have agreed roles and procedures in place – which need to be made clear to all governors to avoid any potentially embarrassing situations.

The other obvious situation in which where there needs to be a clear distinction is in the appointment of the Head and bursar – especially in schools where the bursar is line-managed by the Head (which applies to some, but not all). You should not be directly involved in the appointment of your line manager; nor should you be directly involved in the appointment of your successor, so there will be certain functions of the clerk's role that you will not be able to carry out – for example, in being present at interviews or helping to draw up job descriptions. That said, the procedures and arrangements for such matters nearly always fall to the bursar in practice.

None of the above problems is impossible to solve, but you will need to go though the implications of being the clerk very carefully with your Head and governors, so that there are agreed arrangements in place for those moments when there might be a conflict of interests for you. This is as much for your sanity as for the good of the governing body.

Interestingly, the 2010 ISBA membership survey showed that 80% of bursars were also clerks to their governors. Of the 20% of bursars who weren't also clerks, there were, in many cases, sound reasons for this; perhaps the school was part of a livery company or trust, and thus they would provide the clerk.

Chapter 10

People: legal issues that bursars may encounter

Bryan Login

'Surround yourself with the best people you can find, delegate authority, and don't interfere.' (Ronald Reagan)

If only that happened in the bursar's world! Unfortunately, finding the best people is difficult enough in itself, but retaining them, and ensuring that *they* do not 'damage' your reputation or pride, is a tough challenge. You also have a duty to ensure that *you* treat them fairly and that you do not 'damage' their pride, from the moment you make contact with them to the day they receive their gold watch.

This chapter will cover some of the processes and problems that you may come across during the recruitment process, right through to the management of the employee's exit – whether that is by resignation, retirement, redundancy or dismissal. In addition, it will cover the plethora of human resource issues in-between: issues that may, of course, pre-determine which route of exit they take. Finally, it will touch upon other legislation that could (no, will) creep up and bite the unaware. We are, of course, talking about health and safety, whilst not forgetting the risk to be avoided at all costs: corporate manslaughter!

Recruitment

Recruitment and selection decisions are among the most important decisions that Heads and bursars make on behalf of the school. Get it right, and you complement the future success of the school: get it wrong and you risk failure. It is therefore vitally important that schools should have effective recruitment and HR procedures that, among other things, ensure that all new staff are safe to work with children. So, cover the basics by having a good job description and person specification: these are vital in selecting the right person-fit, job-fit and organisation-fit.

Then send the right message in adverts, by stating how committed you are to safeguarding children (especially by stating that a CRB check is essential). Of equal importance is to make sure that your advert, and for that matter the whole recruitment process, is non-discriminatory in every way. The Equality Act (2010) has made this issue even more significant: avoid any reference to race, age, sex, disability or religion.

You should also ensure that one member of every interview panel has attended the safer recruitment training. Next, use an application form and do not accept just letters or CVs – the reason being that undesirable applicants can avoid certain areas in their own crafted letter or CV. Make sure that references are sent out in a timely manner, and that they are returned, checked and verified before the interview. The verification is an indispensable part of the process.

Check qualifications, and investigate gaps and anomalies. Lastly, make sure you ask for a medical declaration, but only *after* a conditional offer has been made – and make sure someone entitled to do so (in order to comply with the Data Protection Act) looks at it, and refers it up the chain of management if there is a decision to be made about whether that person is employable. Bear in mind, too, that the Equality Act (2010) states that you must make 'reasonable' adjustments for anyone with a disability.

Finally, do not forget the other pre-employment checks that might catch you unawares. You will want proof that the employee has the right to work in the UK, and so you will need to see a passport, or a visa, or a work permit (if the applicant is a non-national). If the job requires qualifications, make sure you see original certificates and driving licences and, if applicable and if it is your policy to employ only such staff, to confirm General Teaching Council membership for all teaching staff with QTS (Qualified Teacher Status).

Safeguarding

> *'So much of what we call management consists*
> *in making it difficult for people to work.'* (Peter Drucker)

It may seem sometimes that well-meaning interference by the authorities has the unintended consequence of making it difficult for people just to get on with their jobs. Never is this more apt than in the area of safeguarding. Although covered elsewhere in this book, it is worthwhile emphasising here too that it absolutely fundamental. Since we are involved with the education and wellbeing of children, it is vitally important that we understand the intent of such legislation.

Safeguarding procedures, incorporating Criminal Record Bureau (formerly List 99) checks are designed to ensure the 'wrong' people find it (very) difficult to associate with children without someone raising the alarm. There are two basic rules: first, ensure employees, and regular volunteers, have an enhanced CRB check, usually *before* they start working with children, and second, that they eventually register with the new Independent Safeguarding Authority (ISA) or its successors.

The Single Central Register

In order to pull the recruitment and safeguarding procedures together, there is, as you would expect, a register! As part of the government's safeguarding initiative, schools have been under a duty, since 1st April 2007, to maintain a Single Central Register (SCR). The SCR requires schools to record the dates on which they carry out identity and qualification checks, checks on List 99 (or the Children's List as it is now called) and, where relevant, CRB checks, and also the right-to-work-in-England checks on all new appointees and staff in post.

The importance and accuracy of this register, and the tenacity of record-keeping on personal staff files, cannot be under-estimated. Any Ofsted or ISI inspection will start (and possibly finish) with this document. The format is available widely, and the time and effort to make sure it's always up-to-date is an investment well-made.

Employment law

Having successfully recruited an employee or volunteer, you now need to be aware of the spectre of employment law breathing down your neck. One thing that will be absolutely crucial in dealing with any subsequent employment law issue will be a properly constructed and signed copy of a staff contract.

There are many versions available, and you should make sure that your HR department (assuming you have the luxury of having one, but if not, your school secretary/bursar), has employment contracts for all employees, and that these are regularly reviewed. Every time you have an issue with leave, sick pay, notice, or whatever, it's the terms and conditions document, or contract, that you will have to refer to and be guided by.

This chapter will now canter through a number of principles, enshrined in employment law, which should keep you on the straight-and-narrow – although you need to bear in mind that legislation in force at the time of writing this chapter is subject to regular updating and change.

The National Minimum Wage

There are various rates for apprentices, 16-17 year-olds, 18-20 year-olds (the 'Youth Development Rate') and over 21s (Adult Rate). The rates change every year, normally in October, and you must pay at least the rate for each age group. This will normally affect work-experience schemes, cleaners and catering staff.

The European Working Time Directive (EWTD)

The EWTD is a directive from the Council of Europe (93/104/EC) to protect workers in the European Union. Adult workers cannot be forced to work more than 48 hours a week on average – normally averaged over 17 weeks. You can however work more than 48 hours in one week, as long as the average over 17 weeks is less than 48 hours per week. If an employee is aged 18 or over and wishes to work more than 48 hours a week, s/he can choose to opt out of the 48 hour limit, but this must be voluntary and in writing. It cannot be in the form of a blanket agreement with the whole workforce.

Statutory Sick Pay (SSP)

Check your employee's contract to see how many days' sick pay you have agreed to pay: it will normally be graduated, depending on how many years the employee has been with you. If there is nothing about this in the contract, you will be obliged to pay SSP for a maximum of (currently) 28 weeks. You can insure against absence, and for the cost of cover to replace that absent member of staff, but that said, it will be based on your previous years' sickness rates and it will, most likely, be prohibitively expensive.

Statutory Maternity Pay (SMP)
If you work in a school, the chances are that female staff outnumber the male staff by some margin. It therefore follows that there may be a succession of pregnancies from time to time. There are maternity leave schemes and maternity pay schemes. The employee is entitled currently to six weeks of 90% normal pay followed by 33 weeks of SMP (check the rates at the time). The employee is entitled to her same, or a suitable alternative, job, on return to work. You can also insure for the cost of cover to replace that absent member of staff. It will be based on your previous years' maternity absences.

Statutory Paternity Leave/Pay
The biological partner of the child can apply for paid leave to look after the mother or child.

Flexible Working
Employees with children under 17 or who are carers can ask for flexible working hours. Seek HR advice on how to approach the request: you have to make a decision within a very short period of time.

Managing performance
For the purposes of this chapter, it is assumed that an employee is now settling down into his/her job and is enjoying the challenge. However, how do you know that they are actually contributing to the school's objectives in a meaningful and measurable way? The conclusion is inescapable: there must be systems in place that assess their current performance and promote a continuing high one. In all the better schools there are well-rehearsed systems in place for teachers in terms of teacher competencies, and there should be a system for support staff as well.

The overall system should monitor performance on a regular basis, at least annually or more often if necessary. These may feed into appropriate pay, grade and/or rewards system. However, do not forget that staff will also need nurturing, training and development: pay is not enough on its own. That said, avoid performance pay schemes as they will eventually reward mediocre performance and create disparities between staff, thus becoming a disincentive. Most importantly, your staff require leadership in all its guises, whether that be direction, problem-solving, decision-making or a generous dose of emotional intelligence.

Pension provision

Most teachers will be part of the Teachers Pensions scheme (TP), a statutory scheme (Teachers Pensions Regulations 1997, as amended). This is a government-run defined benefit final salary scheme paying guaranteed inflation-proof benefits at a cost to employers (currently, in early 2011, 14.1%) and employees (6.4%). It is a hugely bureaucratic and expensive scheme; consequently there will be changes in government legislation that affect the nature of the scheme – initially, probably, for new entrants.

Additionally, under recent legislation all employers will need to make pension provision for all employees, including support staff. The legislation provides for arrangements to be phased in, the details depending on the size of the organisation. If you do not operate a scheme for all, speak to a pension advisor and factor the cost into your budget soon, ensuring that there is an employee contribution built in to the offer.

Managing exit

Logically, the final set of issues in terms of dealing with HR centres around managing the exit of staff from an organisation. For most managers this also is the most difficult phase. Whether they leave through natural retirement, resignation, redundancy or dismissal, the departure of members of staff is going to be a traumatic time, for them and for the school.

That is because old assumptions may need to be re-thought; new personal relationships have to be forged and former working patterns fundamentally altered. So do not be fooled into thinking that losing a member of staff is *always* a good thing: there can sometimes be much truth in the old saying about 'better the devil you know'.

Exit from the organisation happens for three reasons: the individual leaves (*ie* resigns or retires); the organisation changes and no longer needs them (redundancy) or the individual is dismissed (by compromise, constructive or otherwise). Be wary of a high rate of turnover in any category, as this may be an indicator of an underlying problem. Remember, too, that it costs a great deal to recruit, select and train replacements.

Resignations

These can tell you a lot about an organisation. Some people will leave for perfectly unavoidable reasons (*ie* following a partner's relocation). Others may leave through dissatisfaction (voting with their feet). Some people may leave because other schools are offering something better. Whatever the reason it would be interesting to ask the question, in order to discover it. (See also the section on constructive dismissals, which comes later on.)

Retirement

This comes to most people – eventually. Given the latest un-affordability of pensions by government, the Default Retirement Age (DRA) of 65 years has gone to be replaced by a more flexible approach: the DRA moving upwards for both men and women leading to retirement by negotiation. This places an onus on the school to make sure that their personnel procedures are up-to-speed – particularly sickness recording and follow-up, capability and effectiveness monitoring.

Redundancies

They change the culture of an organisation completely, according to Jon Akers, chairman of IBM. Downsizing can have a devastating effect on organisations and therefore should not be entered into lightly. However, having decided to institute a programme of staff reductions, there are several methods for achieving the required savings.

One way of avoiding redundancies is simply not to recruit when people leave: a very blunt and not always effective method of reducing staff numbers. Another way would be to ask for 'voluntary' redundancies. However, you may possibly be killed in the rush of applicants, and having to select between individuals will cause ill-feeling amongst those left or those who were unsuccessful. Finally, there are 'compulsory' redundancies.

Whichever route is chosen, the process brings clearly into focus the need to be unscrupulously fair when managing the programme. Seek specialist HR and legal advice, and be absolutely clear about what should happen at every stage. The minimum you have to pay is Statutory Redundancy Pay, which depends on age and length of service; the maximum will be what is written into the contract plus any offer by the employer. Of all the employment law bear-traps, redundancy is, potentially, the most dangerous. Any abuse of the process could mean facing an Industrial Tribunal, which could worsen your financial position further as those made redundant frequently claim unfair dismissal.

Compromise agreements

Another route that is often taken when things are not going well between employer and employee is a compromise agreement (CA). A CA is a contract between an employer and employee under which the employee receives a negotiated financial sum in exchange for agreeing that he or she will have no further claim against the employer as a result of any breach by the latter of a statutory obligation (*ie* unfair dismissal, discrimination or unfair redundancy).

The agreement will only be valid where (a) it is in writing and (b) the employee has received independent advice from a solicitor (or trade union legal officer) who has professional indemnity insurance. As you would expect, there are bear-traps with compromise agreements, particularly in respect of any tax-free entitlement, so take independent advice from either the tax office or a tax expert.

Constructive dismissal

This is an issue that notoriously and frequently trips up unwary employers – including newer Heads, and those such as directors of music or sport, who oversee particular groups. If an employee resigns from his/her job because of the employer's behaviour, it may be considered to be constructive dismissal. But the employee would need to show that you have committed a serious breach of contract and that s/he felt forced to leave because of that breach. Finally, s/he must show that s/he has not done anything to suggest that s/he has accepted the breach or a change in employment conditions.

Dismissal

Finally, we come to the last resort! There are a myriad of reasons why you might have to dismiss employees. Quite commonly it will be because they have broken one or more of the terms of their employment or contract: for instance continually missing work; poor discipline; drug or alcohol abuse; theft or dishonesty; incompetence. As always, you will need to follow a fair and full disciplinary procedure, which should be laid down in your employment handbook/policy, before dismissing an employee.

Beware of trying to 'dismiss' employees who are long-term sick, or who have a disability. If the employee has a disability (which may include long-term illness), you have a legal duty to try to find a way round the problem. If you treat any employee less favourably than any other for a reason related to disability, or if you do not make reasonable adjustments for them in the workplace, you may fall foul of the Disability Discrimination Act.

Employment tribunals

Before leaving the topic of employment law, we should mention ETs – which hear cases involving employment disputes that have not been resolved by other means. While an ET hearing is less formal than a court hearing, the decisions made by ETs are legally binding and must be followed. Cases are usually heard by a panel of three people, called a tribunal – including a legally qualified employment judge.

Currently there is no charge for an employee (or ex-employee!) taking a case to an ET although s/he has three months to make the claim from the termination date of employment or the date of the incident. At the time of writing, a successful claim brought about for unfair dismissal would attract compensation of over £65,000. You may also have to consider the wider impact that such an award would have on your reputation, and on future working relationships. So, my emphatic advice is to avoid them.

On a final note about *any* contentious people issue: make sure you inform your insurance company. First, they may be able to provide free advice, and second, if you forget to tell them, they will not indemnify you should you subsequently try and make a claim.

Health and safety

No chapter on people issues would be complete without mention of the Health and Safety Act. The H&S Act (1974) resulted from the Robens' Report. The report identified that all earlier legislation had tended to be industry-specific, which left over five million workers 'unprotected'. In any case, accidents in all groups were commonplace and something had to be done: hence the H&S Act.

From the outset, everyone should know that the Act is underpinned by a phrase: 'so far as is reasonably practicable.' This means exactly what it says on the tin, so do not ban egg-and-spoon races! Essentially, keeping that 'reasonably practicable' statement in mind, employers have a responsibility to ensure the health, safety and welfare of employees (including pupils), visitors, and contractors.

What is implied in that requirement is that there must be a *positive* H&S culture within the organisation. Accordingly, you need to display the H&S poster and have an up-to-date written safety policy. Regular H&S meetings involving safety representatives throughout the school are also a good idea. You will need to maintain accident books and report some accidents to the HSE (RIDDOR Reports), and then investigate them and react appropriately. Risk assessments need to be common practice for all activities that pose a risk to safety (swimming pools; trips away from the school; PE; science, minibus operations *etc*; and specific, detailed legislation about the risks of fire).

Fear not, there is H&S expertise widely available through specialist firms (who have template risk assessments, available on websites, to adapt to your circumstances), and through insurance companies which will help you to review your procedures. Finally, training is the key thing: make sure that you have annual training for staff to remind them about how important H&S is, and ensure that your key staff have attended at least a basic awareness course for H&S. Your bursar should be, at least, trained to the equivalent of IOSH level.

To end H&S on a high note (!) the penalties for getting this wrong are potentially devastating. The HSE can issue improvement notices or prohibition notices following unannounced visits. Of more concern, the criminal (yes, *criminal*) courts have powers to imprison for indictable offences or award *unlimited* fines.

If that were not reason enough to pay attention to the H&S Act, there is the possibility of a charge of corporate manslaughter. This charge enables a 'corporation' (as opposed to an individual) to be punished and censured for any culpable conduct that leads to a person's death. It was introduced because it is only rare for an individual to be solely responsible for a death caused by having negligent H&S procedures. Far more frequently such tragedies happen because of a poor 'H&S culture' within a 'corporation'.

Good luck!

Chapter 11

'Non-people' legal issues that bursars may encounter

Alison Martin

A dizzy assortment of 'hats'

This chapter complements the previous one, and seeks to cover other legal issues – rather less directly concerned with people – that all bursars will encounter in their careers. It is worth prefacing it by saying that in my experience, nearly every issue that a bursar encounters is ultimately about people, whether it be a pupil, parent or member of staff. Nevertheless, I shall aim to focus on those legal issues, of which there are many and various, that perhaps fall mostly outside the realm of human resources and employment law.

- Most bursars, but not necessarily all, who wear the finance hat will be responsible for ensuring that the Companies Act, the Consumer Credit Act and the Competition Act are complied with by the school. It is probable that most debtors will be parents, and the chasing of the parental debtor through the county courts will inevitably fall to the bursar.
- Wearing the estates hat, the building laws and regulations, Health and Safety law, contracting with suppliers and hiring out to local or national groups will also fall within the bursar's remit.
- The transport hat has a minefield of various laws and regulations to ensure the bursar's day remains varied and full.
- The security hat contains the province of the Data Protection Act; the law and regulations surrounding e-safety for both staff and pupils – not forgetting the issues regarding the use of CCTV – and keeping the school site as safe as possible from local marauding natives.

- Last, but definitely not least, the catering and domestic hats: these also command a raft of legislation including the use and storage of chemicals, environmental health and food hygiene issues.

Beyond that formidable list lie even more challenges: licensing; copyright laws; patents; trademarks and intellectual property; all of which evade an appropriate hat! They find their place in the margins of the daily grind, and they cause deep sighs to the conscientious bursar, precisely because any issues that fall under these headings are so rare that full research is often required each time a problem arises.

The majority of bursars are also clerk to the governors and it falls to them to ensure that governors do not have any conflicts of interest in either their personal or professional lives. A register of pecuniary interests is a must to ensure that the school and the governor are protected from such accusations.

Research

The clue to combating legal issues is, without any doubt, research. The first problem is to identify whether there is a legal issue or not. I am aware of several instances in my own bursarial career when I discovered, several months after an incident, that there were indeed highly important legal issues that should have been given careful consideration at the time. Fortunately the outcome has been such that I did not discover this until much later and merely sent up a few prayers of thanks to the fates that looked after me on that occasion. However, once you are aware of the issue, the first thing a bursar should ask is: are there any specific regulations that cover this issue? In most cases there are, and if you are not sure of the specifics, rapid research is required.

Some bursars like to find things out for themselves, while others will ask for advice immediately. Most probably fall somewhere between the two. Nearly all issues have been tackled by others before, and the interaction between colleagues and other bursars is invaluable.

The bursarial world is, by and large, a friendly one, so my advice would be to seek the advice of others before poring over the small print of the plethora of acts and regulations that exist and apply to the schools' sector. Given this basic piece of advice: ask other bursars, you may, of course, wish to finish reading at this point, at least so far as this chapter is concerned. However, it needs to be a little longer (the editor says so!), so let us endeavour to uncover some of the detail and provide a few examples – both fictitious and factual. I leave the reader to decide which is which.

The finance hat

The chasing of debt offers a fascinating world of lies and half truths. All bursars learn to recognise the habitual 'stretcher of the truth': the parent who is explaining to the bursar why s/he has not yet paid their school bill. The cheque that never quite makes it into the post; the funds that will almost certainly arrive two weeks into the new term when the previous term still remains unpaid; and the most common excuse: 'we never got the bill.'

Perhaps these particular scenarios apply most often to the bursar whose school's capacity is not filled. I have it on good authority, having never experienced it myself, that those bursars whose school has a waiting list never have to wait for fees for more than two weeks after the beginning of the term in which they are due – let alone the following one...

However, it may eventually be necessary to challenge these 'stretchers of the truth' and to act through the courts to recover the debt. At that point you will need to have a full written history of what was promised, both by the parent and you: when, how and what actually occurred or was agreed.

This leads me in a timely fashion to the next piece of advice. Always, always, always make notes! This applies to nearly all issues, but most definitely applies when dealing with parents, their promises and their actions. I am fortunate in that I trained as a shorthand typist and I can more or less type as fast as I talk and/or think. My notes reflect this: they are rarely grammatical, but they make sufficient sense for all to understand the situation.

In the event that I need to provide evidence I am able to forward my notes as they are, rather than having to start from scratch to set out the issues. Notes made at the time are of far more value, both in the legal sense as well as the perceived one, than those made at a significantly later date. With that very specific piece of advice I will dismount that particular hobby horse and return to the issue of recovering debt.

Parents are a fascinating species. I know because I am one, and because my children went through fee paying schools. These parents come in all shapes and sizes and, crucially, in all guises. I have been stunned by the well-dressed, well-mannered and outwardly supportive parent who turns into anything but this paragon of virtue as soon as the bursar mentions the school's debt collection process.

Some take it as a personal affront, having no regard for the school as a business. "Debt collection is such a grubby business," remarked one recently, "surely the school doesn't have to resort to that?" Another may turn to making accusations about the non-delivery of education. This is unfortunately not so rare, so I return to my earlier advice to emphasise fiercely to all teaching staff – and future bursars – that they should make full and effective notes if a parent raises any issues surrounding dissatisfaction with the school's teaching or facilities. In addition, all complaints must be logged in the school's 'complaints' log book, which will be subject to inspection during the school's normal inspection processes.

Whilst on the subject of fees and fee collection, do watch out for issues that come within the sphere of the Consumer Credit Act. Currently a school can apply for a Consumer Credit licence, which enables the school to offer credit. However, while this arrangement may be applicable now (early 2011), recent rumour indicates that it is likely to be withdrawn soon.

The safest course of action is *not* to offer credit through the school. If a parent takes credit (*ie* s/he is a late payer), this does not constitute a breach of the Consumer Credit Act. However, many bursars, including me, will agree a repayment scheme with the parent. This again is not deemed as 'offering credit' – provided that there is already a debt outstanding. However, agreeing to accept monthly payments before a debt has been incurred is deemed as such, and the difference between the two situations may be marginal.

The Competition Act possibly needs no introduction although, as time marches on, the much publicised issue of some senior independent schools allegedly collaborating to fix fees and thereby stifle competition will become a distant memory. It should not be forgotten, though: sufficient to say that bursars should not discuss *future* fee increases with anybody outside the school's own governing body and senior leadership team. It is totally legal to compare and contrast *current* or *historic* fees with other similar schools, and benchmarking of income and expenditure is encouraged as a measure of value for money.

Finally under the finance hat comes the Companies Act. Perhaps it goes without saying that all independent schools require a financial audit carried out by an external auditor appointed by the board of governors. The auditor should be a good source of information, covering both the Companies Act and in providing relevant financial information throughout the year, to aid the beleaguered bursar and, if needed, to advise the board. If auditors are not doing this, the school should appoint replacements!

The estates hat

Where to start, when turning to the estates hat? The issue of ownership, as will be seen later in the chapter, can be hidden in the mists of time. The new bursar would be well-advised to check with the Land Registry to ensure that the school has on file the exact boundaries of the site and a record of who owns what. Make sure that you are fully up-to-speed on existing covenants, and the local development plan. Pursue sensible opportunities to get the designation of land changed whenever appropriate – and engage with planners.

The Health & Safety Act encompasses many spheres, but it also has the advantage of being well entrenched and widely understood. Many professional consultants will offer the bursar advice on the various aspects of health and safety legislation and, if the bursar feels vulnerable in this area, there are many ways of accessing advice. A regular audit is one possibility and many bursars employ a consultant physically to review the school site after which, if necessary, they can instigate a rolling programme to bring the site up to a higher standard.

A word of warning on the subject of consultants and their advice: if you take professional advice, be prepared to act on it. Make sure that all consultant contracts are carefully drawn up, and avoid ambiguous 'joint responsibilities' that can fall between all parties in such a way that none will take responsibility (or incur subsequent liability). If, for some reason, a bursar receives professional advice and does not wish to act on it, be sure that the advice is presented with the reasons for not doing so, at least to the senior management and preferably to the governors, for their approval and ratification of your actions.

Health and safety

Bursars can mistakenly view health and safety as applicable only to the physical safety of staff and pupils on the school site. It is as important to ensure that this applies off-site as well, and especially to include visits, expeditions (both day and overnight stays), holiday camps and the dreaded home-to-school transport. I know of no greater stress than the annual agreeing of the day pupils' bus timetable and dropping off points.

I have had a parent threaten to sue the school because the day pupils' bus changed its route to pick up several new pupils. Had this ever come to court, I doubt whether the case would have been upheld, but in this particular instance the new bus stop was (how shall we say?) in a less desirable part of town and the parents concerned needed to drop their child at least ten minutes before the bus was due to arrive, in order to enable the parents to get to work on time.

They claimed that, by changing the route, and the bus stop, the school had endangered their child, and they threatened to report the school to the social services, citing a breach of duty of care. I countered with the argument that it was possible that social services would consider that the parents were breaching their own duty of care by regularly leaving their child at a bus stop to wait for a bus, regardless of where the bus stop was. In the end the new route proved longer, and the bus had to pick up earlier than anticipated, to reach the school by the appointed hour.

I could recount many issues similar to that one, where the issue resolves itself in the end for one reason or another but where, given another time and place, it just might have blown up into a fully-grown legal issue. Again, I repeat: take notes all the way through such an issue. If the situation turns nasty, providing you have acted in a reasonable and appropriate manner, the courts will support you. Moreover, if you have done so, very often the issue will die or go away.

Taking legal advice

There comes a time, however, when the bursar has no option but to take external legal advice. This may vary according to his/her previous experience and knowledge. Some schools subscribe to legal advice through their insurer's helpline on a wide variety of issues, although this facility is used more commonly for employment issues only. Most bursars form links and create contacts through local legal firms or through their governors with whom they feel comfortable asking for informal advice. I suggest that taking legal advice should not always be the very first port of call: it is expensive, and much is available on the internet.

However for those issues that occur very rarely (concerning such matters as copyright laws, patents and trademarks), or are likely to be outside the regular experience of even the most long-serving of bursars (such as accidental fire damage or a horrendous minibus accident), it is sensible to seek legal advice. Moreover, at times, spending money on legal advice can ultimately save money. Training courses frequently point to the reluctance of new, inexperienced Heads to seek legal advice early enough in a potentially difficult situation: the same may also apply to new bursars – for example, in cases with risks of constructive dismissal.

Difficult issues

Finally, I will recount four examples of difficult legal issues that I either experienced personally or of that I am aware of. These are not necessarily typical encounters; indeed a lucky bursar may have no need of legal advice for his/her entire career. However, they serve to provide an insight into such matters.

Case one

The first involves a fire in staff accommodation owned by the school, which caused immense damage to the tune of over £1m. The fire started in a self-contained flat, rented by a member of staff, above a housemaster's residence. The housemaster was occupying the accommodation free of charge under licence as part of his employment. The other member of staff and his wife occupied the separate flat under a tenancy agreement. Both had to have their own insurance for their own contents, but both properties were insured by the school under the school's buildings insurance.

The day after the fire the school's insurers sent an assessor in, who photographed the site, interviewed the bursar, the housemaster (who had returned from his holidays) and the member of staff and his wife who had occupied the flat.

At first it was not immediately apparent that the school would need legal advice. However, the school's insurers made a claim against the member of staff's insurers under their contents insurance cover. Although the issue was supposedly between the two insurance companies the school had to ensure that the school's insurers were behaving legally and appropriately in acting against the member of staff.

The school's insurers claimed that, as the member of staff's insurance company would not 'come to the table to negotiate', they needed to claim against the member of staff personally. This took several months and much negotiation to come to a conclusion.

Case two

The second instance involved the contractual agreement with a large multinational building company to build a swimming pool. The building was delayed by several months, partly due to the school changing the plans after the contract was signed, and partly due to inefficiencies and poor project management by the contractor. The issue at stake of course was how much each party was to blame for the delays.

A secondary, but by no means insubstantial, issue was that when the swimming pool building was handed over to the school several months late, the walls were out of line; the windows had gaps around them; the roof leaked and the poolside floor sloped the wrong way – so that when the poolside was cleaned, the dirty water ran into the pool rather than into the drain provided. The amount of money in question was sufficient to employ a specialist legal team to negotiate the school's way through to a reasonable solution.

Case three

Another instance when the bursar called for advice from solicitors arose through a dispute over rights of way along a private footpath at the school's boundary. The right for the footpath to be used by local residents had been granted in the 1950s to allow access from a new housing estate to the town's allotments. The agreement indicated that the footpath could only be used for this purpose, but inevitably it had come to be used just as a convenient throughway for local residents. When the allotments were sold for new housing, the bursar decided to close the footpath.

The bursar took legal advice on how to manage this and negotiated with neighbours for their continued access to their rear gardens using a gate with a padlock. Needless to say, the key to the padlock that had been copied to all the neighbours fell into different hands, and the gate was rarely locked anyway. Eventually the school took further legal advice and managed to enforce the restriction, taking the land back into school use.

Case four

I also know of an interesting situation where a school owned a nominally freehold building, which stood on land that was originally leased. However, the lease had lapsed insofar as the date was past the original end date. The same school had also been given other land in the past under a gentleman's agreement, but the said gentleman having died several years earlier, the estate passed to his son and thence on his death to *his* son.

It was only when the grandson inherited the land that the issue became of importance, due to the liability for death duties. The governors reviewed the situation and asked the bursar to sort it out. This proved easier said than done, and the school spent a lot of money on solicitors and surveyors to get a satisfactory outcome.

The school also had many old and listed buildings, as well as pitches that were adjacent to land that was waterlogged and boggy, and acted as a barrier and thus remained unfenced. However the school needed more external sports facilities, and wanted to drain the boggy land. The first issue to be solved was who exactly owned the land and in the end, despite a lot of research and expense, the ownership could not be traced.

Further expense was incurred in claiming ownership of the land due to occupation. However, as it had been largely under water and therefore unused for generations, it was difficult to prove occupation. Eventually it was resolved, although how I am not entirely sure: suffice to say that the only people really to benefit for the many years that it took to solve the problem were the solicitors and their associates.

Conclusion

There are many other issues which could have been included in this chapter, had space permitted. They include some of the more technical aspects of child protection, described in chapters 4 and 10 – especially in relation to parental responsibility; data protection and information disclosure; record keeping and the mandatory seeking of personnel references. The bursar is also responsible for an ever-wider range of matters – from seeing that the school's Memorandum and Articles of Association are regularly reviewed and fit for purpose, to doing all that can be done to ensure that it cannot fall victim to a bewildering variety of scams or money laundering.

It would be fair to say that the bursar's lot is a diverse one, but if there was ever an area of expertise that was likely to trip up a bursarial career, the legal aspect seems undoubtedly one of the most likely. In these litigious times, when parents are well-informed and the barrack room lawyer is in your midst, it is of paramount importance that bursars look before they leap! But you can never prepare for every contingency: successive governments introduce new legislation almost on a six monthly basis, so who can predict what will come next? But that's another chapter.

Chapter 12

Recruiting a bursar

Andy Dorgan

The Head looked out from his study window across the school playing fields, now bathed in gold from the setting autumn sun. Late swallows still swooped for insects above the pristine green, and a common room XI were batting well against fierce local rivals. But the Head was not smiling. His face was stern and grim. He knew that dark clouds gathered in the east and would engulf the school tomorrow, bringing the first cold rains. Winter's chill would soon follow.

However, the Head was not thinking of the coming winter. Now in his tenth year of office, he was well able to cope with the turning of the year; the challenges of new pupils; the darkening nights, even Christmas. None of these had caused him to look so grim. No, he knew that tomorrow he must engage in one of the darkest of all arts that fell occasionally to a Head to perform. Tomorrow, he and the governors had to appoint a new bursar.

His mind went back to that fateful day in the summer term when Peter, the current incumbent, had oiled into his office one morning – shifty, shuffling and obviously up to no good.

"Morning, bursar," he'd said, "shouldn't you be off cooking books or something equally Byzantine?"

The bursar had smiled his oily smile and simpered ingratiatingly.

"I must discuss something with you, Bernard."

He had slowly come round to announcing his intention to retire, and would take no persuasion to the contrary. Apparently he believed that 75 was old enough in the job for anyone.

The Head sat down and sipped thoughtfully at a cup of lukewarm coffee that still festered on his desk from earlier in the afternoon. His eyes were drawn to the red folder on the top of his in-tray: the applications of those shortlisted and due to arrive tomorrow; all bright eyed, shiny and full of ideas to wow the governors, and himself. The prospect nauseated him. He could picture them now: all business suits and smart phones, firm handshakes and eager enthusiasm. The interview panel would be hard pushed to find a personality amongst the lot of them.

He also knew that tomorrow was potentially troublesome, as the bursar was a governors' appointment, rather than his. Whilst it was unlikely that they would actually appoint anyone whom he was against, they might not want exactly what he did. There was a subgroup of governors who felt that what the school needed was an injection of military efficiency. He shuddered at the thought.

Luckily it had fallen to him, or rather to his PA, to draft the job description and person specification: all manner of sins and wriggle room could be concealed in there. True, the documents had been circulated and approved at a full governors' meeting, but how many governors actually read the papers sent out to them, especially such dry, dusty and lengthy ones as these? He leaned back, slightly comforted, and then thought to himself: actually I suppose *I'd* better read the damn things before tomorrow.

As he sat reading through the description of job and ideal candidate, it occurred to him that the governors were obviously looking for some sort of multi-talented SuperBursar. A jack (or master?) of all trades: someone who could whip up a perfect set of accounts, whilst ensuring that the school was spotlessly cleaned daily; catering of mega-gastronome standard permanently on tap, and all employment and Health & Safety legislation complied with even before the HSE dreamed it up – and all that before ensuring that the pigs were all fed and wings groomed.

That was always the trouble with bursars: what did they actually *do*? They could not possibly be experts in all of these areas, so how should a mere Head prioritise when recruiting one? What does the school need? mused the Head. An accountant? A business manager? A site manager? Or an HR manager? Maybe a bit of each?

The job description and person specification were obviously off-the-shelf productions. There seemed nothing wrong with that, as they covered absolutely all the bases. He recalled Peter had said something about getting a copy from the ISBA, and he assumed that this was what he was now reading. He wondered what Peter had extracted, or added. Looking down the long, long list of duties the Head struggled to think of any tasks that could conceivably be added: taking a maths class, perhaps?

The descriptions of tasks began to blur and merge, but he was pleased that he had reviewed the accompanying information and re-read the covering letter that he had included all those weeks ago. He had managed to include some clarity on the lines of reporting and the importance of the relationship between himself and the new incumbent. Yes, on some things they would report direct to the governors and that was fine. The Head knew his own limitations, and also those areas of the school's operation that he would happily leave to someone else.

He turned to read the applications. They came from wide and varied backgrounds and all offered some level of expertise in one area or another. Two were actually bursars already and were the early front runners. Just as long as they're not too weird, he thought.

He arrived early the next day, wanting time to prepare his thoughts for the ordeal ahead. Margaret, his PA, bustled in with a coffee. "We're all ready for today. They should arrive by 9.00. You give them a little chat and welcome until 9.15: usual spiel, you know. Then they go off on a tour: back at 10.00, after which they go into the interview carousel. Task: two mini-interviews and a session with Peter. Then lunch, and full interviews in your study from 2.30. OK? Thank goodness we managed to reduce the numbers to avoid a second day of all this. Still, we haven't sent out rejection letters yet, so we can always go back to the rest if we don't find someone today..."

Without waiting for an answer she hurried out. Margaret was a cross between mother-in-law and matron, and when there were events to be organised she was in her element – as long as nothing went wrong. But then, something usually *did* go wrong, and the Head was thankful that he would be ensconced in the interviews, firmly out of the firing line.

He continued looking through the application details, but stopped after a while and just sat musing upon the coming day and trying to form clearly in his head an image of the new bursar, whoever that might be. Before he realised it Margaret was tapping on the door and popped her head in.

"The governors are here, and everyone else involved in today is ready. Shall I send them in?"

"Yes, yes. Please do, Margaret."

They all trooped in and took seats around the large meeting table that dominated the Head's study. He rose and crossed the room to the top of the table.

"Thank you all for coming, and to the governors for giving up their time. Margaret is handing round a summary of the programme and you will all see that it is a pretty full day. First they meet me, and the Colonel." He nodded acknowledgment to a large, be-whiskered gentleman on his right: Old Boy, long-standing governor and now chair of the finance committee. A trifle pompous on occasions, but basically a sound egg.

"Then on a site tour with pupils. David, are they all ready and briefed?" he asked, looking to his deputy – a large, round and instantly likeable fellow.

"Yes, they are all briefed and ready. They start by making their way to maths and English, then on from there. The guides have been told they need to be returned to main reception by 10.00..."

* * * *

John Smith turned his car left, drove through the school gates and followed the gravel driveway to an impressive front entrance. Obviously a former stately home – and thankfully, he thought, they have looked after it. So far, so good. He had gone through several of these processes recently: after seven years in post as a bursar, he needed a new challenge. His own Head was retiring and the thought of breaking in the successor was more of a challenge than he cared for, especially as he had met the new specimen, who possessed all the warmth of a re-heated kipper.

He parked, and pulled from the passenger seat the pack of information he had been sent. A fairly standard advert, designed not to scare too many applicants off: ISBA standard version if he wasn't mistaken. The information pack was OK, if again fairly standard. Job description and person spec: again off the shelf from ISBA. A school prospectus bursting with the usual lovely, glossy photos of shiny happy pupils; smiling staff and even the Headmaster's dog. He hoped he'd have time to dig behind the gloss a little during the day.

At least there had been a letter from the Head, in which he had managed to sound vaguely normal, which was encouraging. He had obtained accounts via the Charity Commission, but the school had been unable to produce an organisation chart, or to confirm what the actual salary of the post was. This was especially irritating: they surely had to have a figure or range budgeted for, but all they would say was 'competitive'. Yes, he thought, your definition of competitive, or mine?

He never could understand the sensitivity some schools had on this issue. Secretly he relished the thought of being offered a post, turning it down and explaining: "If only you'd stated the salary at the beginning!" Details about annual leave, pension scheme, *etc,* were also playing truant, undoubtedly to be found skulking behind the bike sheds. John hoped this was not one of those schools that thought that working for them was such a privilege that you should probably do it for free. He checked the time and said to himself: "Right, let's go and see."

They were all seated in the Head's study. John looked around at his rivals, a rather typical crop: all business suits and smart phones, he scoffed to himself, and then reached into his own business suit to check that his smart phone was turned off.

The Head was coming across well: a pleasing blend of bonhomie and 'we're going to enjoy giving you a right grilling'. He also actually said this was supposed to be a two-way process, with 'you finding out whether this school is the right place for you'. OK, thought John. Again, so far so good but, not sure about the chap with the enormous whiskers – chair of finance, was he?

The site tour was, well, exercise. It did, however, afford a reasonably gentle introduction to the day. John knew, having been on the other side of the table more times than he cared to remember, that the site tour was usually first, as it gave time for the interview panels to grab a coffee, think up their questions and re-arrange the furniture in the interview room. He was dismayed to find that a presentation was still required – should he survive until the afternoon. No job description he had ever seen for the role of bursar had had 'giving presentations' as a major element; yet presentations seemed to feature in the majority of recruitment days.

The tour also gave a chance to size up the opposition: one other existing bursar; one candidate from business management; an accountant; an obviously ex-military figure and one from building management. All offered expertise in one area or another, but only two had had the all-round experience of working as a bursar.

Before long he found himself in the interview carousel. A collection of interviews and tasks designed to … well, he wasn't sure of the 'design' element. More a collection of shop window events to allow various interested parties to size him up, plus a couple of tasks that someone had probably thought were a good idea.

He'd always found interview tasks a bit hit and miss, and the present one was no exception. As a spreadsheet task, a Year 7 pupil could have done it and as an accounting test, his cat could have passed it with flying colours. He recalled other tests he had done. At the other end of the spectrum, he had once been presented with 50 pages of premises issues and associated cost estimates, and had been asked to draft a presentation on priorities, people involved and project management in an hour.

He wondered whether one day he would come across potential employers who had decided beforehand exactly what they wanted to find out from a test or in-tray exercise and designed one accordingly. Some schools even did full-blown psychometric testing, which was always a really fun way to while away an hour of interview time.

The mini-interviews went well; at least, John *thought* they had gone well. Not too many curve balls from left field that had left him gasping for words like a newly landed fish. He had, however, been asked his hated stock interview question: "What do you consider to be your greatest weakness?" Too easy: "I take on too much myself. If someone asks me to take on a task, I say yes."

"So your greatest weakness is working *too* hard?" He promised himself that one day he'd answer that one honestly with something like "I really should not get so angry with the kids" or "I wish I could give up smoking".

He decided to take a short walk around the site as the carousel came to an end: there was a short gap until lunch. This was quite often the most informative time – just wandering around the site; looking into the corners omitted from the tour; seeing how the pupils behaved towards each other and towards visitors.

Did the staff look happy as they went about their business? Did they challenge the stranger in their midst or couldn't they care less? This school overall left a good impression. Pupils were polite and seemed happy to be here, as well as inquisitive about who he was and what he was doing here. Here for a job! What was he going to teach? "You look after the money – can I have some, Sir?"

He returned to find that a vast expanse of sandwiches and fruit had been provided. He ate little, as he always found that food did not sit well on a stomach awaiting an interview cut. He passed the usual pleasantries and small talk with his fellow candidates, finding out where they had come from, what they were doing now and why they were here. He realised he had some serious competition, and only one of the candidates to his mind not really having a chance. But then you never could quite tell what it was that the school was looking for.

Suddenly the door swung open and the Head and deputy swept into the room as if about to address an assembly. Well, they did have bad news for someone. However, they announced that they would be seeing everyone individually to tell them if they were to go forward to the afternoon. A distinct plus in John's book, whatever happened. He always hated the public humiliation of a group announcement: a cowardly way out, when it took so little time to speak to everyone individually. His own interview was short, just to tell him he was through to the afternoon. The Head smiled as he told him. John could not quite decide if it was the smile of a snake about to strike, or of a soon to be friend-in-welcome.

The afternoon interview was very similar to many that he had been through before. They had taken care to arrange the room so that it seemed less like an inquisition. When he asked them some questions, they were engaged and forthcoming, unlike some he had come across who seemed genuinely shocked that the applicant dared to ask them anything. He watched the Head as much as he could whilst answering questions thrown at him, because he knew full well it was the Head's opinion that would really matter.

And the Head in turn watched him intently, sizing him up and trying to picture this fellow walking into his office in the morning with news of the latest pressing issue. He read and re-read through application, letter and references and looked again at the chap sitting before him. More and more it grew upon him that he could indeed see himself working with John.

The interview came to an end. The Head thanked John and confirmed the arrangements for contact later, once a decision had been made.

* * * *

After all the interviews were concluded, the panel members eased back into their chairs and called for coffee. It always surprised the Head how tiring interviewing could be – no matter how many times one had done it before. And now came the really fun part: the panel's discussion and, hopefully, agreement.

An initial round to discover whom they all had earmarked as number one produced a split decision. The Colonel and two other governors wanted the ex-military chap with the manic smile, who would have them all square bashing in a week. Over my dead body, thought the Head.

The Head and his deputy and one governor wanted John. The Head knew that whilst two of the governors who disagreed could easily be swayed, the Colonel would take a little more working-on. Both candidates were quite evenly matched in qualifications, experience and qualities needed. The Head finally came to his last hope.

"Well Colonel, I'm sure both could carry out the job admirably, but I can see this John Smith fitting in better with the team. I'm not sure I could work with the Captain."

"Major, Headmaster… Major." The Colonel pondered for a long while. Was this worth a damaging split with the Head? After all, the Head had to work with the fellow. "But do you think this chap can carry through the reviews and reforms that we need?"

"Yes, Colonel, I do and I feel he could do so with a more humane face than the dear Major. You must remember Colonel that we have some delicate souls in education."

The Colonel pondered for a while but eventually said: "Very well, as you wish."

A collective sigh passed around the room as peace and harmony were re-established between staff and governors. Thanks were said, and said again, and then the party broke up, still reflecting and discussing the day's events and seeking to reassure themselves that they had indeed reached the right decision.

* * * *

Later that afternoon the Head called John and offered him the post. It always sounded so much less like an offer these days, with all the caveats that were required: "Subject to a health questionnaire, CRB check *etc etc*." But at least John had said "Yes".

The Head got up after the call and looked out across the fields once again. The leaves were turning gold, red and brown, and winter could not be too far away, but the autumn sun shone and the Head could feel a balance returning to his world. It always seemed such a long process, this business of recruitment, and in many ways an imperfect one. However, he had not yet thought of a better way to find anyone he could tolerate having in the office down the hall. Those who had been invited to interview could all have done the job – unless of course the school had made a complete mess of the job description or shortlisting process.

He always felt that the point of the interview day was to find the one whom he could work with: the one who was going to fit in. That was the crucial factor: who would fit in *here*. He realised many of his fellow Heads would have gone for someone more forceful and dynamic. No, he could provide the dynamism himself, and moreover, he realised his own shortcomings. He often needed a calmer, steadier and more cautious voice to tell him when to calm down, when not to do something: a steady hand. He knew what the school and its leadership team needed, and John could fill those gaps.

That was always the key. What exactly did the school need: accountant; building manager; general manager; dynamic, innovative or more balanced and solid? The one who fitted in should be the one who brought the required experience and expertise, but also the right personal qualities. All schools, and all leadership teams, were different. The key was to find the right piece of the jigsaw that would complement the team as a whole and not just mirror oneself or fit a pre-conceived idea of what a bursar should be – whatever that might be.

Margaret bustled in with a coffee and pile of letters not dealt with as a result of the loss of a normal working day.

"Well, Headmaster, a successful day I hope?"

"Yes, thank you, Margaret. I think he's going to fit in really well."

Chapter 13

The bursar in a boarding school

Mark Taylor

'The bursar is the synovial cushion in the elbow designed to reduce irritation.'

To start with, I wondered where on earth I might begin, but the realisation increasingly grew on me that I should draw directly on my own experiences as a bursar. In doing so, one thing should be emphasised straightaway: what follows describes the aspects of the job that occur specifically in boarding schools – but all the challenges and opportunities described in other chapters also apply.

Overview

Since 1993 I have been fortunate to have worked in four outstanding schools, ranging from a grant maintained school to a prep school and two HMC schools. All of them have had some degree of boarding, either full or weekly: Cranbrook; Dulwich Prep at Cranbrook; Bedales; and now The King's School, Canterbury. In this chapter I draw particularly on my experience at the last-named.

There is no doubt that the regulatory requirements since 1993 have increased dramatically. A little research in this area quickly reveals that when I started working in boarding schools, there were not much more than a handful of such demands. By contrast, today we have over 300 regulations, most of them distinctly prescriptive.

I therefore suggest that the bursar in a boarding school has an extremely important part to play in the educational community. There is an important balance to maintain. On the one hand, the bursar must ensure implementation of the stringent legislation. On the other s/he must be able to allow the house staff the space and ability to run their houses. At the time of writing the air is filled with optimistic talk of de-regulation, and the possibility (through primary legislation) of ISI taking over the inspection of boarding schools from Ofsted. Time will tell but such developments would not be before time.

Boarding house finances

Historically there seems to have grown up a tried and tested financial structure for boarding houses in which a greater degree of centralisation and oversight has been the order of the day compared with what was once the case. At King's Canterbury the day-to-day house finances were all centralised within the accounts department in 2008. Financial guidance is issued and there are two house sub accounts:

- Capitation grants. Each year an allocation is made to houses, based on the number of pupils in that house. The funds are used for day-to-day expenditure within the house such as newspapers, DVDs/videos *etc.*
- Entertainment allowance. This is used for entertaining parents only.

Other more specific areas of expenditure are covered through centralised budgets. These are furniture and furnishings; TV licences/satellite; purchase of new televisions and IT equipment; new pianos. There is an annual procedure that checks the house requirement ahead of setting the annual budget.

We undertake monthly accounting, which provides us with the discipline to analyse the expenditure on a very frequent basis. It introduces a further administrative burden, but for me it works well and keeps me focused.

The other critical financial factor is the condition of the boarding house: refurbishment is expensive, very important and needs clear planning and programming. I have experienced various models of this, and I fully appreciate the importance of engaging with house staff at the earliest opportunity.

A housemaster or mistress is appointed to a house for a fixed tenure of 12 years; each 12-year break is taken as an opportunity to give a boarding house a major refurbishment from top to bottom. During the interim years there is a period of inspection, with maintenance and minor upgrades undertaken on an 'as and when' basis. Having just finished a complete tour of the boarding houses I remain amazed at how well this system operates. Facilities appear well looked after and treated, and much care has been taken in the choice of hard-wearing but attractive furnishings.

Regulation, regulation and regulation

In March 2002 the National Minimum Standards (NMS) for boarding arrived in the bursar's in-tray, detailing the minimum standards required for all boarding schools. In all, 52 standards were provided and these became the benchmark for boarding inspections. During summer 2010 (close to the General Election) an updated version of NMS appeared, and thankfully the Boarding School Association (BSA) quickly picked this up and alerted member schools as well as providing a summary of the changes.

It was quite interesting to note that the latest NMS carries the caveat that: 'We anticipate that these standards will need updating within a year to reflect the policies of the new government. For this reason they are only available in electronic format.'

This is certainly code for 'watch this space'. Meanwhile, for me the implementation of NMS has been quite a challenge. A number of the requirements are very prescriptive, with little room for variation. How do you implement the required ratio of washbasins and WCs to students, without stripping the character from a building that needs to have a homely appeal? Standard 42 requires that dormitories are of adequate size, and where there is a disagreement over whether a room is too small or overcrowded, the term '*adequate*' is defined within the School Premises Regulations 1999.

Largely thanks to strong representation from BSA, the major revisions proposed in spring 2010 were scrapped. BSA spent quite a significant time advising on possible tweaks to the old NMS and thankfully Ofsted has adopted (*pro tem*) the BSA suggestions. The even newer revision of NMS is threatened to be a year or two away and it is good to know that BSA is very much on the case.

Relations with staff

I have always found it fascinating to watch how a boarding school operates. The pace during term-time is highly intense. Events often proceed at quite a gallop, as 52 weeks' worth of work is squeezed into 33 or 34 weeks. Activities start from 8am and continue until lights out, with pastoral care provided for 24 hours a day; we have 750-plus employees on the payroll.

There are many different ways in which bursars operate in boarding schools, and realise that the way I operate will be wholly different to others. But in varying ways I have come to realise, in each of the four schools in which I have worked, how crucially important the bursar's role is.

This awareness has two overall aspects. First, I fully understand and appreciate that the role of the bursar's department is to support the academic function of the school, and not to try simply to apply an inappropriate commercial template. Secondly, I am very keen to be as much a part of the academic community as I can; I believe that an effective bursar finds it much easier to support the direction of the school if s/he is able to appreciate the major concerns and issues and all those who work in it.

Schools differ, of course, in their attitude about which meetings a bursar should attend. As well as the senior management team meetings (SMT), I think the house staff meetings are very important in really helping to understand the complexity of the boarding operation. My bursarial career started in 1993 as deputy bursar at Cranbrook School; part of my responsibilities there included the oversight of matrons and of the administration of the boarding houses. Becoming a boarding house tutor for a spell did much to help me understand how a boarding school works and how a bursar can actively support the boarding operation.

Health and safety

No discussion about being bursar in a boarding school would be complete without a comment on health and safety (H&S), fire precautions and catering. An area of constant debate in many schools is just how the H&S requirements can be met effectively within a boarding house. A housemaster or housemistress will normally have responsibility for H&S delegated to him or her by the Head, and s/he should therefore carry out a risk assessment of the boarding house, to ensure that appropriate measures are taken to minimise or prevent risks, and that staff employed at the house are appropriately trained.

The H&S requirements do not seem set to ease in any way in the years to come, and if there is one area of constant teacher exasperation it seems that H&S is it. My own experience has been that if the requirements on house staff are clear, and if they appreciate that they have the back-up of the estates department, the basic requirement of H&S are not difficult to achieve. That said, there are many areas of challenge.

One such area I constantly wrestle with is the portable appliance testing requirements. The testing of school equipment is very straightforward. However once you extend it, as you must, to the students' own appliances, you have quite a task. At King's we ask parents to ensure that personal electronic appliances that are brought back to school are tested before arrival.

In addition we undertake our own yearly check and testing of appliances. It is always interesting to see what this reveals: for example, silver foil and other bits of metal used instead of fuses, *etc*. The inescapable conclusion is that this remains a constant area of risk. We have good procedures in place to cover all other eventualities but how do you monitor the condition of personal equipment that can be brought in at any time? You can only be constantly vigilant.

Fire

Fire in any school with boarders is always a major worry; the stakes – and the requirements and worry – quickly escalate. There is a general legal requirement to take adequate fire precautions, the scope of which includes:

- Fire doors, fire escapes, detection and alarm systems and extinguishers, all regularly inspected and maintained.
- Evacuation procedures tested regularly by fire drills.
- Systems for safe storage, regular collection and disposal of waste.
- Furniture that is made of materials that comply with the upholstered furniture regulations (Source 5).

I was delighted recently to be visited by the Kent Fire Brigade. They explained that they hadn't been on a detailed tour of our site recently and wondered if we might consider a joint exercise with them. They were at pains to explain that they would not be assessing our procedures but were more keen to test their own. We thought that this was an excellent idea, and the plan was to undertake a live joint exercise with pupils in a boarding house, with the aim of testing both school and fire brigade procedures. It struck me what a useful exercise this would be for any school, and I would recommend getting in touch with your own local fire brigade office to explore the possibilities.

The importance of good food

I was staggered when I worked out that we provide approximately 18,500 meals a week through four dining rooms – and I have certainly learned that this is a critical area to get right. The provision of good, healthy food does much to help lift the spirits of any school, and it is remarkable how important this is perceived to be, both by existing and potential parents and pupils. With such a focus on provision of food, King's has engaged the services of a qualified nutritionist to review and scrutinise the menus across the site. This has undoubtedly helped to develop a good culture of healthy eating. Indeed, I was brought up short when one of our catering staff commented on the lack of green on my plate at lunch…

Some key legal implications

Another topic that merits discussion is the whole legal area of Terms and Conditions (T&Cs) of entry for pupils. I have been very grateful to Veale Wasbrough Vizards who, over the years, have kept me alert to new requirements as well as inadequacies in my own T&Cs. I thought that maybe a review every few years might do. In fact I have found that I needed to undertake *at least* a yearly review over the last four years. As a result, I am now the proud owner of T&Cs that have over 100 conditions. So I suppose that regulation does sometimes have its benefits!

As my brief is to reflect on the boarding side of the bursar's job, probably the most constant source of debate around T&Cs is the change from boarding status to day. The T&Cs are very clear on this issue: a term's written notice is required before a pupil changes from boarding to day status, and in default a term's difference in fees will be payable in lieu. Where a boarder is deemed to be a disrupting influence and is asked to cease boarding permanently and become a day pupil, if his/her parents live abroad this could well be tantamount to requiring the pupil to leave the school.

Once, the review of T&Cs was completed just in time for the new September intake and I was very grateful for the advice that, for all the remaining parents, I simply needed to send them a copy of the new version with the next fee bill run, asking them to read it and keep it safe. If the bill is then paid following receipt of the amended terms and conditions, the new T&Cs are deemed to have been accepted. That said, it is crucially important to ensure that all is done to draw parents' attention to the amended T&Cs.

Crisis management

> *Crisis: 'Any incident which has the potential to affect short or long term confidence in an organisation, or which can interfere with its ability to continue operating normally.'*

Crisis management is another area of challenge. In a community like King's, of more than 1200 students and some 750 staff, it is likely that there will be accidents, times of difficulty and even tragedy. However careful we are in the way we conduct ourselves; however clear and effective the guidelines for staff and students are, things can go wrong. A crisis may occur on the school site during the school day when we are all available to deal with it. It is just as likely to occur away from school and out of hours – perhaps involving people on school visits either in this country or abroad.

However much you may feel that crises are not things on which you should dwell, they do happen and you need to be quite clear in advance just what your plan of action will be. Parents and the emergency services will certainly expect it and, in extreme cases, media involvement might make it essential. Although every crisis will be unique, involving different people in different situations, there will be common threads that need to be planned for.

Having experienced a few minor crises I am very much of the view that advance planning is critical: having the opportunity to think through 'what if' scenarios quietly, rather than as the crisis unfolds, is more than helpful – and, once the thinking-through has been done, the conclusions should be incorporated into a comprehensive, written disaster plan.

While I was at Bedales I was fortunate to have a very experienced governor who had been charged with oversight of school risk. His advice was that we should, as a matter of course, undertake business continuity tests based on certain scenarios each year. We identified the following to start the process:

- The need to close the school at short notice – how would we do this?
- Loss of electricity across the whole site.
- Loss of oil and gas across the whole site.
- Loss of mains water into the school.
- Large section of staff and pupils not able to get to the school.
- Loss of telephones.
- Incident in which we get adverse PR – how would we react?
- Large scale staff and student sickness.

I found these exercises extremely helpful. We also agreed that each crisis that actually occurred would be carefully reviewed and scrutinised as well.

Summary

Inevitably, I have highlighted only a fraction of the areas in which a boarding school bursar might be involved and I hope that at least something I have expressed may be helpful. Many other facets of the job might have been included: for example, when I started bursaring in 1993, it was in a world pretty much before email had caught on.

Above all, I have witnessed in that time a dramatic change in the bursar's overall responsibility. The nature of the job seems to have changed, particularly due to the mammoth increase in legislation. Given my sense is that things are not going to get any easier, thank goodness that we have such a competent, professional and proactive ISBA Secretariat to help guide and advise us through the myriad of regulatory and other requirements.

Chapter 14

Schools as charities: what difference does charitable status make?

Ray Maher

I will never forget the look on my friend's face when he realised that the independent school I worked for was a charity. As we all know, charity is about helping the poor – so he was intrigued to know how an organisation, which (as he saw it) had been established to help 'rich kids' take over from their parents in society's pecking order, managed to get charitable status and all its associated benefits. Was this another tax loophole for the super-rich to reside comfortably in, alongside their pad in Monaco, whilst monitoring their bank account in the Cayman Islands?

There is a common understanding of what it means to be 'charitable': giving voluntarily to, or helping, those in need; kindness; benevolence; tolerance in judging others; loving one's fellow man. As a parent with three teenage children I appreciate their needs, particularly for tolerance, but I also readily accept, along with others, the distinction between parental responsibility and charity. So how does a school funded by parents become a charity?

Misconceptions are all too common, and they are not the exclusive preserve of those outside the independent sector, looking in. I have been involved in commercial and charitable initiatives with the education sector since 1992 and have been fascinated by the journey. I hope my perspective will provide some insight into the broader implications of charitable status for strategic decision-making within a school.

If you are looking for a comprehensive practical summary I recommend *England and Wales Charities – A Practical Guide* by the UK200Group.

Although not geared to schools specifically, its 23,000-plus words are an easy read to understand the basics in all areas. If you want a school-specific technical manual, you should find the ISBA website an enjoyable read. However, be warned: my computer began to smoke when I asked it to count the words in what is *the* resource for school administrators.

The key to getting under the skin of this issue lies in appreciating:

- What is charitable status? Why can it include independent schools?
- What is the Charity Commission? What does it do, and what can schools expect?
- What are the practical implications of not being a commercial school?

What is charitable status? Why can it include independent schools?

I may have been influenced by working alongside a very enthusiastic historian and Head Master. However, I make no apologies for indulging my interest in the history of English charity law for two reasons. First, because education provided by church schools played such a vital role in the process. Education was at the heart of the development of charity law itself. Secondly, because going back to first principles is often the only way to retain some sanity around the changing moods as to what constitutes Public Benefit.

Making sense of the distinction between 'charitable status' and 'being charitable' in English law hinges around the response of the state to our Christian heritage. The former describes the status conferred on the private organisation by the state to serve laudable public purposes. The latter is described by the Apostle Paul, in his first letter to the church at Corinth, as the greatest of Christian virtues. The law evolved largely to encourage and protect public spiritedness in order to maximise the resources applied to welfare provision.

In essence, the state has an interest in the welfare of its people and wants them to be housed, healthy, educated, *etc*. Historically it has sought, and continues to seek, to encourage and fund welfare provision in all its forms, through a combination of public and private finance. Welfare charities seek donations, but they are often encouraged to charge those who are able to pay, and who benefit from their services, in order to garner in welcome additional finance.

That government should identify closely with the charitable sector is natural, given the definition of charity as serving public purposes. One may say that the state takes responsibility for many issues that might otherwise be left to charity, and our history to the present day has been an ebb and flow of state responsibility. More often than not the state of the public purse has acted like a moon to this tide.

In Britain we customarily talk of voluntary organisations (or sometimes of the voluntary sector and voluntary action). Within that grouping, charities form a distinctive part of the sector, defined by their particular public purposes. They are bodies serving the community: not just volunteers or co-operatives serving mutual private ends.

Charities today may take a number of forms. The main ones are:

1. charitable companies, which are corporate bodies with charitable purposes;
2. associations, where a group of individuals come together for a charitable purpose; and
3. trusts, with trust deeds setting out the charitable purposes for which their resources must be used.

The four core ingredients of any charity irrespective of its form are:

1. that its purposes are recognised as exclusively charitable in law;
2. that it is established for the Public Benefit;
3. that it enjoys independent governance; and
4. that it practises non-profit distribution.

Rooted in the mists of time

Charity is a distinctive and long-standing branch of English law. Surprisingly there was, strictly speaking, no precise definition of terminology until 2006 – despite the fact that charity law has a very long history going back to a time before the first Act of Parliament in 1601. It needs to be understood in the context of the common law tradition that citizens have a right to form associations without needing state authority.

Thus voluntary bodies do not need permission to exist, and indeed they do not need a specific legal form. Charity law and related legislation exists, in principle, as much to protect charities as to regulate them. Why would charitable activity need protection? Why would private citizens need assurances from the state about independent governance? The establishment of my current employer, King Edward VI School Southampton, in 1553 gives an interesting backdrop to the first Charity Act in 1601.

English almshouses providing housing for the needy have existed for around 1000 years. It was not until the Renaissance period that the first translation of the Bible into English arrived, produced by a University of Oxford professor named John Wycliffe, shortly before his death in 1384.

By the late 1500s printed versions were widespread. This period saw dramatic changes in the church across Europe and consequently in education in England. Movable type was invented in 1434 with the first book, the Gutenberg Bible, being printed in 1456. Gutenberg's invention laid the foundation for the commercial mass production of books. The success of printing meant that books soon became cheaper, and ever-increasing sections of the population could afford them. More than ever before, books enabled people to follow debates and to take part in discussions of matters that concerned them. Hus, Erasmus, Calvin and Tyndale were all dominant personalities in this context.

Then, in 1517, Martin Luther criticised the power and practices of the Catholic Church by nailing his 95 grievances to the door of the church in Wittenburg. Many people joined his protest and became known as Protestants. By 1527 the efforts of John Knox and Thomas Cranmer had ensured that this Reformation had spread from Germany to England.

Henry VIII's break from Rome with the Act of Reformation in 1534 had a damaging effect on education. The dissolution of the monasteries in particular, deprived many communities of educational provision. For Henry, this plundering of the wealth of the church was a means of filling his coffers, but the financial respite that this afforded him was only temporary. By the mid 1540s he was short of money again, and at that stage his eye turned to the wealth of the chantries.

A chantry was not a building, but an endowment for a priest to be based within a church. His function was the singing of masses for the dead. However, chantry priests did not confine themselves to this basic function: many conducted schools, and keeping a school was sometimes required by the terms of the original foundation. By the mid-Tudor period there were somewhere between 2000-3000 chantries, so their wealth was a valued prize. The dissolution, however, was justified in religious terms, as it was no longer appropriate in a Protestant society to sing masses for the dead. An Act of Parliament was passed in 1547 and in the following year the chantries were abolished as, indeed, were many of their associated schools. One such chantry was attached to St Mary's Church in Southampton.

The dissolution of many religious houses and endowments meant that schools were disappearing quickly. and yet this period – the reign of Edward VI in particular – has long been trumpeted as a great era of new educational foundations. How can this be? The truth is that it was all done by sleight of hand. Many 'new' schools were simply re-foundations.

These foundations were not the result of government policy. Both new foundations and re-endowments were normally achieved through the efforts of local citizens who re-purchased the property from the government. The schools were in fact local, private initiatives: very few gifts came from the Crown.

Whether King Edward VI School Southampton was a new foundation or a re-foundation cannot be resolved, but what is clear is that its foundation had a lot to do with the efforts of the rector of St Mary's, William Capon, and very little to do with those of Edward VI. In 1550 the rector's will stated:

> I give and bequeathe to the towne of Southampton one hundredth poundes to the erection maynetenance and fyndings of a gramer scole there perpetually.

The mayor and recorder, together with four 'ancients' were charged with carrying out his wishes and had to provide £10 per annum for a schoolmaster. Application was duly made to the Crown and Letters Patent were eventually issued on 4th June 1553.

Our present legal status (along with that of many other schools) derives from an Act of Parliament in 1601 that reaffirmed the charitable framework in order to tackle post-medieval social and economic difficulties by providing assurances and protection, thus harnessing the commitment of the public spirit.

The Industrial Revolution prompted a further upsurge of philanthropic activity in many new forms, embraced within the developing tradition of voluntary and charitable activity. The British welfare state redefined the relationship after the Second World War, when the state took over responsibility for much welfare provision: social services; health; housing; education and so on.

As its costs burgeon, the reliance of government on charities, to deliver public good, increases. With this increasing reliance has come recognition of new areas of work as being charitable (the original list included just education, religion, the relief of poverty and 'other' purposes beneficial to the community). Now areas such as community development, animal welfare and environmental protection are recognised as charitable goals.

Until 2006, it was legally presumed that educational charities were always established for the public benefit (*ie* that a sufficient section of the public was able to benefit from the purposes of each charity). The Charities Act 2006 removed the *presumption* of public benefit from charities – including educational ones – and the burden of proof now falls on the charity. Yet the public benefit derived from charitable independent schools has been recognised for centuries, wherever the burden of proof lies.

What is the Charity Commission?
What does it do, and what can schools expect?

Accountability and audit

The ultimate legal accountability of charities is to the High Court, which protects the use of charity money to ensure that it goes to its public charitable purpose. The Crown, as *parens patriae* ('father of the nation'), is the ultimate enforcer of charitable trusts on behalf of the public, acting through the Attorney General. The Commission's role (and, indeed, its origins in 1853) is ultimately to act as a streamlined administrative alternative to the oversight of the High Court, and to carry out the oversight function on behalf of the Crown.

It has an overriding duty to use its powers to enhance the ability of the trustees to achieve their charitable purposes, and in a way that will increase public trust and confidence in charities. It is not allowed by law to administer charities itself, but has broad regulatory powers to direct the application of charitable property. It can only intervene to remedy misconduct or mismanagement – with its powers being geared towards putting things right rather than imposing sanctions. The Commission also has a facilitating role in helping charities and trustees to take courses of action which only the Commission can authorise.

Whether the extensive Commission guidance for fee charging schools, following the Charities Act 2006, has strayed beyond its remit into the modern politics of social mobility is likely to be tested in the courts – particularly the Commission's insistence that means-tested bursaries must form the core on which any public benefit is built. This is an interpretation held by the Commissioners that many leading lawyers and academics believe has no legal foundation – at least, not yet.

In practical terms of course, bursaries are costly, pushing up fees and thus ultimately reducing the range of children able to benefit. This in turn results in an overall reduction in social mobility. Increased opportunities for the poor will be paid for by the rich, with any reduced social mobility falling on aspiring middle class parents priced out of the market. Finding objective commentary free from political bias on this topic is as easy as breathing under water.

Annual and Summary Information Returns (SIRs)

These are straightforward and best completed online. The Commission website is very user friendly, and designed so that the ordinary member of the public (or fee-paying parent) can see at a glance where his or her money has gone. The figures you input on the annual return (from your audited accounts) are automatically put into various graphs and pie charts, that immediately come up when you search a charity registration number.

It also graphs how closely you submit returns against deadlines under 'financial history'! In the same vein the SIR is effectively a self-evaluation. It is completed by you, in layman's terms, setting out what the objects of the charity are: what you have achieved in the last year, and what your targets are for the coming year. It is important to check your previous SIR so that what you state as having been achieved in the year ties in with the targets previously stated for that year. You can enhance your mastery in the art of meeting targets by delaying completion of the SIR until just before the deadline.

Accounts and trustees' report

The Guidance for Independent Schools on Public Benefit Reporting under the Charities SORP 2005 (with specimen annual reports and accounts), otherwise known as the 'blue book', is *the* book to get hold of as a definitive accounting guide.

Your auditors will guide you through the Charities SORP 2005 (Statement of Recommended Accounting Practice), Charities (Accounts and Reports) Regulations 2008 and related matters. The Commission has issued an 'ideal' trustees' report for a charitable, fee-charging independent school. It is onerous and repetitive. Few schools have tried to follow this as very little is mandatory. The 'blue book' example report is very different and somewhat briefer.

King Edward VI School Southampton (No. 1088030) seeks to mirror the Commission's ideal from the year ending 31st August 2009. Such returns can be found on the Commission's website. The returns may favour those who have a good story to tell and who wish to market their school through all public literature. Whatever the case, it is important that you keep a clear and consistent message in all public documents.

Practical implications of not being a commercial school

Strategic factors (ethos and funding considerations)

It is important to say at the outset that I am biased. I believe passionately in the private sector; in the individual; that being charitable is about being generous with your own time and money. Being generous with other people's money doesn't strike me as an act of charity. I have been heavily involved in PFI projects, working closely with major banking groups and public sector bodies on joint urban regeneration initiatives. I left that world after ten years to join a commercial education company with 12 schools in the UK and nine overseas. I believe in the ability of a loosely regulated market place to minimise inefficiencies in matching supply with demand.

The underlying ethos of a school is critical to the experience of the pupil and, however well camouflaged, is ultimately and unavoidably determined by the primary objective of the principal funder(s). Generalisations can be unhelpful when trying to understand a specific commercial or charitable school, but this chapter will give clear pointers, and as is often the case in the classic crime thriller, the answer lies in following the money.

Charitable schools have education as their primary objective. Commercial schools will have education as their secondary objective. For obvious reasons, private owner(s) who have vast wealth and no interest in the financial return on their investment in buying or setting up a school (*ie* profit distribution) tend to set up charitable schools. This status gives them integrity, ensuring that no one can be in any doubt about their primary objective or mission.

Consider the following:

> **Our Mission (2010)**
> Our roadmap starts with our mission, which is enduring. It declares our purpose as a company and serves as the standard against which we weigh our actions and decisions.
> • To refresh the world
> • To inspire moments of optimisim and happiness.
> • To create value and make a difference.

Is this the mission statement of a school? In many ways it could be, but in fact it is the one developed by the Coca-Cola company. Some may argue: does it matter whether or not that company really does think the world is a better place if a lot of their particular brand is consumed? Some may say, "I like it. It makes me feel happier and inspired". On the same basis can't we argue that a school is a school is a school? After all, the parents (and pupils) in a commercial independent school are just as demanding about the quality of educational provision. If that demand is met to their satisfaction, the motivation of the supplier is irrelevant.

	Charity	**Commercial**
Fee setting	The cost of the educational provision required to meet the need/demand divided by the number of fee payers over any given period.	What the market will bear.
Class sizes	Optimum class size to maximise learning and development.	Optimum class size to maximise profit.
Quality of provision	Optimum provision based on supply needs of catchment area.	Minimum required exceeding next best competitor in catchment area.
Investment	All funds raised are invested in the school	Profits are distributed.

Whether the ultimate decision-maker in a school is an educationalist or an accountant at heart makes no difference to the quality of provision.

Yet intuitively, this doesn't feel right, and this is borne out in practice. The primary financial motivation fundamentally alters a school's priorities and focus, and particularly if funded by the financial markets, will prejudice decisions in favour of the short term. The significant fixed cost element exacerbates this short term-ism.

It is important to recognise that a charity is always constrained by default to remain within what the market will bear. A common temptation is to allow yourself to become detached from the markets relevant to the different areas of your operation. Trying to operate in isolation from the market environment can result in painful corrections. Good charity management requires a commercial edge, but crucially the energy of the senior management team of a charitable school, including that of the bursar, should be directed towards the 'child' and to delivering the 'service', thus resisting the mathematician's instinct to reduce the process, in a high fixed cost business, to bums on seats. In a commercial setting, unless the bursar is the sole owner, he is unlikely to be afforded such luxury.

Why do charitable schools behave commercially? Again, to get the answer we need to focus on how the school is funded. High gearing levels can often give undue leverage in the decision-making process to debt funders. Historically, charities were not permitted to borrow, but pressures on the legislatures to give greater discretion to trustees to manage their affairs led to changes. The first statutory provision for borrowing against land was introduced in 1855. It is clearly in the interests of the state to allow flexibility for funds to be levered into meeting a welfare demand that otherwise might need to be met by the state.

Entering into debt to take advantage of an opportunity in an area of provision is often done based on business plans that look to pay back over the longer term, reducing gearing back to previous levels whilst leaving an enduring legacy. From past recessions it can be seen that the parameters agreed with debt funders can suffer a sudden seismic shift as the funders move to protect their own interests ahead of those of the school.

There is a cost/benefit to be weighed up here, and there are few charitable schools that are debt free, but it is wise to steer well clear of the tipping point. Normal risk management rules apply. It may pay to lock into long-term fixed interest options, if there is less room for manoeuvre or greater uncertainty in other parameters impacting the charity's ability to service the debt.

Conclusion

Thus comes to an end this journey through part of the maze of issues that are very specific to a school that is also a registered charity. Chapter 16, Lord High Everything Else, raises some important flags on the technical issues for the charitable school – such as objects, risk, reserves, investments and taxation. You can then follow up on specific areas using the practical guides mentioned above.

In England charitable schools have a unique history that has placed British education as *the* global educational brand. It is completely unparalleled, and it is at the very top of every emerging middle class wish list for their children, worldwide. British International Schools? Now there's another story!

Chapter 15

Managing ICT and its spending

Bruno Delacave

In a chapter on ICT, I hope that you won't mind my starting with a definition from Wikipedia in which it describes it as:

> All technical means used to handle information and aid communication, including computer, telephony and network hardware as well as the necessary software.

This relatively tame and wide-ranging definition hardly seems to do justice to the challenge that ICT represents in a school environment, even though the term 'ICT' only entered the National Curriculum in 2000. So why, unlike discussions about a school's anti-bullying policy or the new library, which are welcomed, does discussing ICT feel like a move to the 'dark side'?

It may help us to gain an appreciation of the significance of information and communications technology if we ask ourselves a question: what would be different in a school if ICT as we know it today was absent? There would be no phones, no emails. Writing documents would take much longer, and keeping track of addresses and pupil records would be harder.

Lesson plans, carefully prepared, couldn't include video and internet data feeds, and registration would be done manually, while all homework would be handwritten in exercise books. Many of the useful websites that deliver vital reference information and teaching aids would not exist. Cyber bullying could not happen; nor would the relationship networks, so adored by many pupils today, exist. There would be more desk space; power consumption would be lower; the cost of education would be less and rooms dedicated to PCs could serve other purposes.

This very brief summary goes a little way towards explaining how far ICT has infiltrated almost every aspect of school life, and why it is so important to manage ICT well in order to ensure that it benefits all schools and their pupils and staff.

Despite ICT's importance, it appears that the approach taken by many schools is remarkably nonchalant. Depending on the passion and aptitude of a small number of individuals, schools have developed a range of technologies: some homemade, while others are 'industry standard'. Their common feature, however, is that they are cobbled together and operated, often with minimum investment, as well as local circumstances allow.

Senior staff are happy for the ICT technicians to shoulder the responsibility of the ICT function: they are also generally satisfied as long as emails; Microsoft Office; access to the internet; printers and photocopiers keep working. What an expensive way to manage some documents, and to have a broadband connection! This is reflected in recent surveys of schools and charities, which have revealed an astonishing lack of any discussion about ICT within development and strategic plans. Why is ICT such a problem?

The trouble with ICT

First, I suggest that ICT is developing at such a pace that governors, Heads and senior management teams in schools often don't understand the changes, or fail to perceive their potential benefits. To make matters worse, they feel unable to explain how the school benefits from the often high investment in ICT which, when its annual costs are presented for approval, leads to cries around the governing body table of: "Really! Why that much?"

Secondly there is a wide gulf between the ICT culture and that of educationalists. The ICT professional adapts to change on an almost daily basis because Moore's Law is driving processing ability up, and costs down – which in turn means that cheaper and better devices and technological solutions are constantly being developed.

ICT professionals are also engineers, lovingly managing a delicate and occasionally temperamental machine that nobody worries about when all is well, but for which the ICT team gets much grief when the slightest thing goes wrong or whenever they have to take the system down for maintenance or upgrade. The teachers and support staff, by contrast, have little or no concern for the technological solutions embedded in ICT as long as it works when they need it and there is support to help them when they get stuck.

Thirdly, the people developing the technology are often young and willing to experiment. Contrast that with Douglas Adams (of *Hitchhiker's Guide to the Galaxy* fame) who suggested a set of rules that describe our reactions to technologies: namely that (1) anything that is in the world when you're born is normal and ordinary and is just a natural part of the way the world works; while (2) anything that's invented between when you're 15 and 35 is new and exciting and revolutionary and you can probably get a career in it; and finally (3) that anything invented after you're 35 is against the natural order of things.

Most decision-makers in schools are over 35! It is seldom that the advocates of ICT have a place within the governing body, the SMT or at heads of department meetings – which is foolish, given how much a school will probably be spending on ICT and the potential solutions and possibilities that ICT can offer.

Fourthly, the pressure for better ICT is seldom driven by teachers, and for good reason. Only the latest generation of teachers has received extensive ICT training and is itself well accustomed to, and capable of, maximising its use and benefits. Instead, teachers will have developed, through trial and error, teaching and pastoral techniques and approaches that they successfully deliver. While ICT-based tools and content can be integrated at the fringe of their teaching plans, wholeheartedly to embrace technology in teaching would require an extensive re-think of how teachers educate pupils: a re-assessment that they probably lack the time or expertise to undertake.

Such features as remote learning; on-line assessments; artificial intelligence; spaced learning; collaborative working; portals and interactive exploration could open huge possibilities in the methods brought to bear on a child's education. They could also better prepare them for the 'real' modern world which, despite being feasible from an ICT perspective, is today rarely discussed in school.

Finally, for many people, ICT is hard to understand, as its language is full of abbreviations and weird technical speak that hardly induces it to receiving high expenditure and playing an essential strategic role in the wider life of the school.

It is within this challenging context of conflict, complication and regular change that decisions about the ICT team and ICT procurement need to be made. It is not an easy task, which is why it has traditionally been left to the ICT technician – and maybe to a few teachers or support staff who have an interest in the subject.

However, such are the advantages, risks and costs to ICT that it is no longer acceptable for governors, Heads and SMTs to take such a narrow view: the control over ICT has to return firmly into the heart of any school's core operational and strategic processes. How might this happen in practice?

The overall framework

In any journey it is essential to fix the destination first. With ICT in particular, a clear mission or purpose is vital, as every aspect of the ICT operation will be built around objectives that must be measurable and meaningful, and for which named individuals can be held responsible. It is unlikely that teachers and support staff will feel capable of defining the kind of ICT solution that will help a school to achieve its educational goals, let alone of making the careful and often complex decisions about competing technologies and how much to invest.

This is where the help of key governors with strong ICT skills should be sought – as should that of a small number of dedicated staff, supported in all likelihood by the advice of expert external consultants. Such a working party would ideally have the opportunity to visit other schools; speak with reference sites; audit what is currently available within the school; attend industry conferences and be sufficiently well-informed about the school's own goals and objectives to be able to form a view about what is necessary and achievable.

Once a strategic objective has been agreed, the school must determine what is to be achieved and address how to embed those recommendations into every aspect of the school, whilst at the same time minimising the risks of failure.

It is at this point that building the right team is essential. As we shall see a little later, whether an in-house or external solution is adopted, a head of ICT is an essential recruit. ICT will have two key components in the school – namely the networking department and the educational ICT department. The networking department is responsible for 'keeping the lights on', and for purchasing, installing, running, maintaining, monitoring and improving all the hardware and software that enables the school's ICT activities to function, including that required by the support staff, such as facilities and financial software.

The educational ICT department will be focused on how the educational strategy in support of teaching and learning is selected, implemented and used. Some schools appoint a senior teacher as head of ICT, while others have a member of SMT, often the bursar, appointed head of ICT to whom the head of networking and the head of educational ICT report. If the service is entirely out-sourced, it is still important to employ a senior ICT person, particularly with regard to educational ICT.

All heads of networking will need to have a deep understanding of how the ICT system works. This will include network integration; operating systems; internet connections; mobile services and data storage and security. They will be capable of fault-finding; monitoring performance and understanding how to defend the school's system. Their skill and experience will enable them to play a key role in writing an ICT risk assessment, and in mapping out a delivery plan.

They will be closely involved with the SMT in deciding the terms of the networking department's service level agreement to the rest of the school, in which they will specify how and when things will get fixed, repaired, upgraded, backed up or improved. The problem is often whether a school can find such a person at a salary that is compatible with other staff, and whether that person will be prepared to remain in the post for some time if the school's ICT is not really being developed.

The head of networking will also require regular on-going training, and must be someone in whom the school has absolute trust. The Head, bursar and SMT should recognise these challenges and appoint carefully.

The other factor to consider when appointing such a person is that their working conditions will in all likelihood be quite different from those of their colleagues. S/he will have to be contactable at all times and be able to work flexi-time, so as to run updates and maintenance programmes at weekends, during the evening and outside normal school hours.

The head of educational ICT will be much more focused on what the ICT functions made available by the networking department (hopefully, in close collaboration with them) can do for the school. The educational ICT department will be looking for curriculum software; data resources; freeware and much more in order to help the teaching and learning.

Heads of networking and educational ICT will work together on school-wide software such as the MIS; the telephone systems; emails; internet security; CCTV and blacklist websites in order to provide a safe and secure environment. Together they will decide on key school solutions in relation to the needs of staff and pupils, for which they will try and provide these services.

The educational ICT department will also have an important role to play in advising the school on such matters as whether pupil testing is to be done on-line; whether learning is computer-based; how to track pupil progress; how to develop effective communications with parents, and how the efficiency and effectiveness of teaching can be enhanced by ICT.

The head of educational ICT should be assisted by a number of other staff and pupils, as well as outside consultants. The post-holder will work closely with the school's head of ICT, the child protection officer and the teacher(s) responsible for pastoral care to ensure that Data Protection Act and child protection legislation is properly applied, and that the school's ICT policies and procedures meet the requisite standards.

Together, the heads of networking and educational ICT should develop the ICT risk assessment, which will be a vital document in order to determine the speed and cost of ICT development. For each area of risk they should assess how serious the problem could be if it happened; then consider how likely this might be to occur, with a resulting prioritisation of risk and severity.

In this risk assessment, they will take into account important issues such as physical security; data security; business continuity and data back-up; email security; and the handling of mobile and other third party devices connecting to the school's network. The risk assessment should also ensure that there is proper budgeting and system monitoring for which appropriate reporting channels are required.

Taking ICT into the wider school

Much of what has been described above could be regarded as preparatory work before actual purchases are made, and the school's ICT service is developed to its optimal level. It includes many elements on which most of the staff and governors might not feel able to comment.

However, staff quite rightly have strong views on many of the specific uses that they make of ICT, such as who should be able to see the emails they write; who checks which internet sites are being accessed from the school; how easy it is to get a class going in a lesson using laptops; and how the school would manage if it lost its internet connection. These questions will cause operational and budgetary decisions to be taken that will significantly impact the workings of the ICT function.

At this point, opening the ICT debate to the wider audience of staff, pupils and parents is to be encouraged. Bringing a wide group of stakeholders into the debate about the extent of ICT provision, the service levels and its potential benefits and challenges, will create the necessary support for ICT within the school without which it is hard to deliver the desired benefits. These school-wide working parties will also have an important impact on the timing of developments in ICT provision and can play a key role in helping to roll out new or improved ICT solutions.

A key decision is whether to create an in-house team responsible for managing all the school's ICT, or to retain the support of a managed service provider who is responsible for delivering a package of services in agreement with the school. The recent developments in virtualisation and cloud computing are likely to reduce the gap between these two choices. Specialist advice should be sought in order to assist a school in this important decision, as it is still unclear as to which is likely to be the better outcome.

The solution will depend on many factors, including whether the school has staff capable of running the whole ICT function; whether the school is looking for a standard solution rather than something more bespoke; whether the school can achieve price competitiveness through its own purchasing channels; whether e-enabled teaching and operations can be better developed and implemented in-house or through the service provider, and whether the school's staff have the time to dedicate to the running of the ICT service.

To assist the heads of networking and educational ICT, it is suggested that a school's ICT department either employ or train its own staff to provide a range of essential support services. For the networking department this would include fault management; repairs; assisting with technical problems; providing first-line support; helping new staff and pupils to become accustomed to the school's systems; and monitoring usage and service levels.

In the educational ICT department, duties would include training staff, pupils and parents in the use of the available ICT networking; developing think-tanks to suggest improved solutions and methodologies; and helping with the use of such things as Whiteboards and class Twitter groups or developing material for iTunesU.

It would be desirable to have a regular bi-weekly meeting with the networking team to ensure that all service levels are being satisfied; risks monitored; budgets respected and system threats evaluated. Meanwhile the networking team could meet twice every term to report on training plans and the ideas they are developing. The two departments should hold a termly joint meeting, to be attended by the governor responsible for ICT; the Head and bursar; the heads of networking and educational ICT; the director of studies or similar and any key outside ICT provider – particularly where managed services have been contracted. This meeting should report to the finance and general purposes, or other similar, committee of governors who will be keen to establish that the goals as set out are being satisfied in the time specified and at the agreed cost.

On that final note, it is recommended that costs are controlled by treating the three core ICT cost areas separately: namely, those of personnel, hardware and ICT software. Decisions about selecting the right ICT staff can be taken only once the core ICT objectives have been defined, in order that a job description and person specification can be established as required by the safer recruitment provisions. It would also be advisable to create a job description for those members of staff assisting with training, think tanks and working parties in order for them to have clarity about their roles within an ICT context.

Making the right buying decision

Turning to the purchase of hardware and software, no ICT investment should be possible unless it clearly fits into the agreed strategy (the so-called product risk). The temptation to buy 'toys' for the ICT team to experiment with should be avoided if at all possible! It will be important to determine who can suggest what should be purchased, ensuring that such personnel are independent of the suppliers and that all reasonable alternatives have been considered.

The supplier risk will need to be considered, particularly if the school is managing its own ICT, even though in a fast-paced industry finding the right supplier can be a time-consuming exercise. The terms of the purchase; the licences; the contract and whether the school can honour what it is being asked to agree to must be carefully analysed, especially where the amounts become substantial; governors will need to counter-sign.

It is also essential to have the time, and the relevant market information, with which to make the right decision. The ICT team must ensure compatibility of the new hardware or software with existing ICT services. Care will have to be taken where leasing or agreeing to make deferred payments, as these may impact on the school's banking covenants, and the means of financing will play an important role in agreeing a fair price.

The bursar and the school's auditors will want to satisfy themselves about whether the purchased items are to be capitalised or expensed; in which period and how they are to be treated for VAT. The maintenance of the purchased items will be carefully evaluated, and a financial and operational plan to replace the items at the end of their useful lives will also be necessary. Hopefully, with all the steps mentioned, carefully prepared prior to making the purchase of goods or services (especially those of higher value), the school will buy the right items at the right time, for the right price and will then find that they work as expected!

The ICT team should also seek feedback on use of its products by staff, pupils and parents. This is where cheap online survey tools can provide a quick and cost-effective solution. If the implementation of this is successful, it might be beneficial to involve the school's PR advisers in communicating the initiative to the school's stakeholders, and to the wider community. Finally, the effectiveness of the ICT solution should ideally be benchmarked with other, similar schools or organisations, in order for the school to know when it needs to be contemplating a new service or upgrade.

Conclusion

ICT is already well-established within schools, but often in a somewhat understated and inefficient manner. This prevents them from obtaining the full benefit of their investment, as a result of which resources are wasted and barriers to ICT development are created. By bringing ICT development back to the heart of a school's strategy; deciding how best to use what it offers; building teams and holding consultations around those concerned; and carefully purchasing and monitoring its implementation and use, many benefits accrue.

Chapter 16

Lord High Everything Else

John Pratten

Taking Gilbert and Sullivan as my starting point, it would not be too far off the mark to compare the bursar with Ko-Ko, the Lord High Executioner in *The Mikado*. I especially like the opening lines: 'Behold the Lord High Executioner: A personage of noble rank and title; A dignified and potent officer; Whose functions are particularly vital.' I do not, however, see the staff common room joining in the chorus: 'Defer, defer, to the Lord High Executioner!'

Anyway, my 'lot', and it is a particularly 'happy one' (to mangle yet another G&S chorus line), is to sweep up everything else not covered in the previous chapters. This provides a sobering reminder: that the bursar's role tends to be a less glamorous one than Ko-Ko's, and certainly one with more of a catch-all nature: more like the title enjoyed by another great character from the same opera, Pooh-Bah: Lord High Everything Else. However, according to one encyclopaedia, a Pooh-Bah is 'a pompous ostentatious official, especially one who, holding many offices, fulfils none of them'. So let us not push the analogy too far...

I have some ten topics to cover, so I'm going to have to flick the brevity switch firmly on and try to hit a happy medium between large and small schools. Please remember this is a personal view, but if there are three words that a bursar should remember, they are delegation, delegation, and delegation. Actually a new word has entered the lexicon and will crop up quite often in the diatribe, and that's 'compliance'.

Catering

Every bursar will tell you that the secret of good catering is the catering manager. Whether such a person is employed in or out of house doesn't matter. My personal preference is for a real 'foodie'. You can't beat the catering manager coming out of the kitchen in whites at lunchtime to check that the food is being presented on the plates properly. Discipline has to be good in a kitchen; so when you hear plenty of "Yes, chef, no chef, Headmaster's scallops will be two minutes chef", you know everything is running well.

In or out of house catering is very much a personal preference, and there are advantages and disadvantages to both options. I have tried both, but have always preferred the latter. My own experience is that in-house is undoubtedly cheaper – provided, of course, that it is well-run – but the use of a catering company is a whole lot less worry for a busy bursar.

For a start there are no direct problems about HR, environmental health or financial control, leaving the bursar to crack the whip over the quality of the food and its value for money, and to pay the bill. It is only fair also to say, however, that at many a bursars' area meeting the pros and cons of in-house have been hotly debated by supporters on both sides. Interestingly, the figures show a 50-50 split between in-house and outsourced catering in independent schools.

A couple of quick hints on selecting a suitable catering company. First, work out your catering budget and ask the contenders to tell you how creative they can be with money. To go for the cheapest is always a big mistake. Go instead for the company that will deliver what you want. Secondly, check the contract carefully for hidden costs (especially mark-ups on capital purchases). Make sure that the budget is transparent, and that the catering manager has the necessary support for major school functions. There is a very helpful template on drawing up a catering tender document on the ISBA website.

Insurance

You can never have enough insurance! Bursars do not have a great deal of choice about which broker they use. There are only a few major players who understand the industry, and who cover all the areas that need to be covered. To my mind there's not a lot between them and although there might be an attractive price to lure a new customer, prices tend to even out in the end.

Just make sure that the following boxes are ticked: property damage; cash; business interruption; assault and personal accident; employer's liability; public and products liability; professional indemnity; governors' liability; crisis communication; terrorism (if you have high profile pupils or buildings); legal expenses; hirer's liability; travel; fidelity guarantee, and of course motor insurance.

I would highlight a couple of areas. Legal expenses insurance (especially the employment cover) is a must, as I use it without fail several times each term. It doesn't matter how trivial the question – and even if you know the answer – make sure you have consulted the insurers and received a reference number. If things go wrong in the future, your costs are then covered.

You would be right in thinking that I omitted to do this once and regretted it! I also have extra travel insurance for the SMT as they tend to travel the world whilst recruiting. This precaution was certainly useful in the early part of 2010 when that unpronounceable volcano erupted, stranding our deputy head in the Far East.

Lettings

I fully appreciate that it is only schools with boarding facilities that will be able to make a sustainable income from letting out their facilities during the holidays. Schools with sports halls should, in most cases, be able to cover at least their outgoings and to break even. Some schools I know are lucky enough to make more than that. However, I think it is perfectly possible that every school should be able to make some supplementary income in one way or another.

I have also heard that bursars have a huge problem with their living-in staff complaining about holiday lets disturbing their off-duty time. I'm sorry but that does not cut any ice with me whatsoever. The school needs the income; staff do not pay rent (or if they do, it can be refunded over that time), and the accommodation is provided for the 'better performance of their duties' during term-time. A simple addition to their Licence to Occupy will resolve any problems as this agreement is not part of their contract.

Don't forget that if you are 'providing education', you do not have to charge VAT – so invoice the staff costs separately if you are sub-letting to a language school.

School shop

When I first started as a bursar, I thought the school shop would be a good source of extra income. Subsequently I had what is, for a bursar, a Damascene moment! I try now to use it as a facility to provide our parents with the school uniform at a reasonable cost, and the pupils with some essentials at the same price that they would pay in the high street.

As bursar, it is part of your moral job description to see that the parents and pupils are treated fairly, and this includes keeping the cost of the corporate items of uniform to a minimum. Try to avoid shirts that have to be made specially, and use white shirts that parents can buy in Tesco or M&S; keep an eye on the sports department getting parents to buy 1st XI rugby shirts; and fix an upper limit on what pupils can purchase from the school shop without explicit parental permission.

If your shop is outsourced, make sure that you have a line in the contract that gives you control over the amount charged to parents for uniform. It is far too easy for the proprietor to keep putting up the prices until the school blazer could be made to measure more cheaply in Savile Row.

Trading companies

Trading companies are useful, but any loopholes for charities in this respect are closing fast. However, if a school has taxable supplies in excess of the registration limit, there are advantages to running some activities through such a company. Rather than trying to squeeze 14 gallons into a pint pot I suggest discussing such things with your accountant, but I would add the following health warning: schools that are charities could breach their charitable objects if they carry out a trading activity other than those of the primary objective of the charity. So to run the sports hall through a trading company is fine, but to run an online betting shop for bursars is not!

To quote from the *Bursars' Guide*: 'Most educational activities that are exempt when carried out by the school will be taxable in the hands of a trading company. This creates planning opportunities, but also traps for the unwary.' In other words, get some advice.

Transport

Maintaining the minibus fleet would be a breeze if it weren't for the pupils and staff. Some pupils have a propensity for destruction from the inside, while the staff are doing their best to destroy the vehicle from the outside! I exaggerate, of course.

One of the recent, and best, appointments that I've made has been the transport manager. His scrutiny of the coach hire in the school has saved his salary and much more besides! I know the old saying that costs come in on two legs, and I am conscious that not all schools can afford such a beast, but with our minibus fleet going hither and thither; the exigencies of uncoordinated school fixtures; and the myriad of maintenance problems that occur daily I consider it a wise investment.

One problem around which we've recently circumnavigated our way was the tricky question of how many staff are permitted to drive minibuses; the younger the teacher, the less chance there is of them having the D1 'tick' on their licence. However, if the minibus is below a certain weight, and it is only for local work such as sports fixtures, they can drive it. The conclusion is that one should hang on to the older minibuses just for this purpose.

Cleaning

I could sum this section up in one sentence: 'Employ a good housekeeper.' The benefits of having an efficient person in charge of the cleaning cannot be overstated. If he or she could be fluent in several of the Balkan languages, that would be huge help! Bursars have their part to play too, however, for example by keeping an eye on the relationships in the cleaning department. It was not so long ago that it came to light that several of the cleaners were sharing a house, and the heady relationships between siblings and associated partners caused a huge ruckus.

Caretaking

Caretaking will mean different things to different schools. In a day school it probably does what it says on the tin. In a boarding school it will most likely be combined with some other job to make best use of that person's time and the free accommodation.

Risk management

It is quite incredible how this culture has grown over the last five or six years. It wasn't so many years ago that we were all trying to convince the staff that there was a logical reason why they had to complete a risk assessment to visit the local swimming pool; since then it has become second nature, and all the generic risk assessments have become freely available on the internet.

Risk management is still a hot topic, especially with ISI and its compliance requirements. One thing should be emphasised: it concerns a great deal more than health and safety, even if H&S is often its most time-consuming and high-profile component. Every governing body should insist on a comprehensive risk register, which is regularly reviewed by (for example) the estates or F&GP committee – although such groups exercise only delegated authority.

Ultimately it is a full board responsibility to ensure that the register exists and is fit for purpose. It should include assessments of a wide range of potential risks embracing, amongst other things: political change; financial meltdown and failure of other corporate and financial institutions; mishaps to key personnel; lapses in compliance; natural disasters; legal and reputational risks; changes in the market; and the impact of educational trends.

It will also, of course, include risks associated with H&S. Where H&S itself is concerned, every room in every building has to be risk-assessed for fire and other hazards. The time this takes should not be underestimated and, yet again, you need a good consultant if you can't afford to employ a risk manager. I've opted for the former, as once things are up to speed it is then only a matter of annual monitoring.

I suggest an annual audit conducted by an outside agency. This has several benefits: you can have the constant worries (CDT, science, *etc*) checked regularly; you can highlight particular worries each year (school visits, maintenance, security, trips and hazards, *etc*); and the report can form the basis of your annual report to governors.

It is also worth reorganising the filing of your risk assessments, so that they are ready for the ISI and Ofsted. Many of the compliance issues in the regulatory requirements and national minimum standards overlap, and both inspecting organisations require sight of risk assessments. A properly prepared system will ease the scrutiny.

Investment management

If you're fortunate enough to have some investments, may I refer you to the *Bursar's Guide*, which is the source from which I am going to précis this information! No better place to start than with a quote from Juliette Roberts of HSBC Investment Banking, who wrote the relevant chapter in the guide:

> Any investment policy for schools will be determined by the legal constraints; terms of any trusts that exist; operational requirements of the school; and prudent application of investment expertise to the current and future financial obligations of the school. As with any other institution, schools have immediate operational requirements for such items as salaries and books; medium term liabilities for, say, extra staff or building refurbishment; and long term liabilities for major developments such as new buildings or a new series of educational courses.

I commend to you a ten-year cash flow: it is a stunningly efficient way of determining the shape and size of the school. It identifies the years when perhaps the fee increase might have to be larger than normal, thus enabling you to spread that increase over a number of years. It can also serve as a brake in an over-zealous or impetuous Head.

I also recommend, for bursars in schools with sizeable investments, that you encourage your chairman to recruit the services of an investment banker to the board: they are probably in need of friends at the moment, and you can pick one up fairly easily in Klosters during the ski season.

Taxation

Trying hard to follow the *Reduced Shakespeare*'s format, I shall attempt to sum up taxation in some 300 words! I've got some good news and some bad news:

The bad news:

VAT – we have to pay it and, in the majority of cases, there's no way to claim it back, except if you build boarding accommodation, in which case you can then avoid paying it. Luckily, as a charity we do not have to charge VAT on fees, since education is granted exemption under Group 6, Schedule 9, VATA 1994. If you want any more detail, look it up!

And, if you have your head in the regulations, then also have a squint at the following items: mandatory registration; self supply of buildings construction services; change of use of a building to a non-qualifying purpose; reverse charge services now applicable to overseas agents (that was a painful amount of money in this year's budget!). The whole area is a minefield and non-accountancy-qualified bursars should seek advice from their accountants.

Benefits in kind – beware, especially when it comes to staff accommodation. I think it very sensible to get your accountants to carry out a 'benefit in kind' audit of all the living-in staff. This will identify any staff who may not be compliant with the school's 'for the better performance of your duties' requirement.

Once you have identified these individuals, HMRC will have to be contacted to obtain an opinion, which can be logged against that teacher. Please don't forget that 'opinions' can differ widely on the HMRC Advice Line. I will mention here a bit of a shocker that should be included in the Licence to Occupy. Make sure there is a ban on running any sort of business from a school property that is allocated for the better performance of someone's duty. If the Revenue get to hear about it, not only will they start charging the market rent as a benefit in kind to that particular occupant, but also to *every* occupant on the campus!

Peripatetic music teachers can be a real problem especially where 'self-employed status' is concerned. I know it's a risky strategy but it would be sensible to invite a team in to discuss the tax treatment of the peripatetic staff. We certainly did, and the Revenue were extremely helpful.

The good news (my headache's better):

Other commercial activities

By and large a school should try to utilise as many of its facilities as it can during school holidays (and, if possible, during the term as well). An obvious way of doing this for all boarding schools is the advantages of the holiday let (substantial added income: a topic covered earlier in this chapter) and it will be equally obvious to all schools which have a sports hall that significant income can be generated from them.

However, every effort should also be made to gain income from more peripheral activities: letting out classrooms in the evenings; use of sports pitches; wedding receptions; in fact, *anything* (well, almost anything legal and decent) that might come your way that can boost the income to the school.

Conclusion

The load that falls within a bursar's bailiwick has increased hugely over the last decade or so, and that fact is universally true, regardless of the size of school. So the bursar of a small prep school will have almost as much to deal with as one of the bigger, well-endowed establishments (whose *alumni* were recycling arrows at the Battle of Hastings), whilst at the same time having to unblock the drains: something that his better-endowed counterpart may be able to avoid.

The burden of 'compliance' is greater than one might think, from ensuring that the hot water does not exceed 43°C to having nervous palpitations about the Central Register and keeping count of the risk assessment mountain.

Lord High Everything Else is not so wide of the mark!

Chapter 17

Getting the most out of the ISBA

Paul Motte

In considering what support ISBA can offer you, it is worth reflecting firstly on the charitable object of the Association: the advancement of education by the promotion of efficient and effective administration and ancillary services at independent schools.

Of the eight associations that together make up the Independent Schools Council (ISC), ISBA is similar to the Association of Governing Bodies in Independent Schools (AGBIS) in that it is the school, not the individual bursar, that is the member of the association, although the bursar is usually the school's nominated representative. The five Heads' associations, on the other hand, have different criteria, whereby the individual Head is the member of the respective association.

This differing criterion of membership regularly leads to debate within ISBA as to whether the bursar or school should be the member and I shall return to this debate later. But in recognising that it is the school that is the member, getting the most out of the ISBA should not be limited to the nominated representative – the bursar – but to the school community more generally. This applies particularly to governors, other members of the senior management team and staff for whom the bursar is responsible.

Although full membership of the Association is restricted to schools in membership of ISC, ISBA offers associate membership to other schools, including overseas schools, provided that the school is recognised as an educational charity. Membership is subject to the recommendation of the executive committee to the annual general meeting.

As a bursar who has served in schools in full membership of ISC, and now in an educational institution that is not in full membership of ISC, the only difference I notice in the benefits I receive from membership is that I cannot vote at the Association's annual general meeting. All other services and benefits provided by ISBA are available to me and my current college. It is my view that both the college and I would be less effective without membership, and I would probably have to subscribe to various organisations and periodicals to gather the width of information necessary for me to operate efficiently.

Before considering the services provided by ISBA, let me reflect for a moment on the role of the bursar. In the maintained sector the term 'school business manager' is more widely used than 'bursar', because it is seen to more accurately define the role, whereas the use of the term 'bursar' does not always sit comfortably in the sector. Meanwhile, in the independent sector, the number of bursars is slowly declining: we see more business managers, operations directors, resource managers and finance directors. However, 'bursar' still remains the preferred job title in three-quarters of our schools.

Whatever the differences in job title, and the differences in our schools, we share a lot of issues and concerns. While we may enjoy individual support from our governors, and from colleagues on our own senior management teams, as far as issues affecting our individual establishments are concerned, there are times when, if the ISBA did not exist, we would need to create it! There are very few problems that we face in our day-to-day operations that have not already been experienced by one of our colleagues. We need an organisation that brings those experiences together, and makes the lessons learnt available to us all.

So, the first and most important benefit from membership of the ISBA is the general support that we get from each other; from the Association's secretariat; and from the significant network of contacts that have been fostered on our behalf. That support is available through a number of specific initiatives and projects that are detailed below.

However the day-to-day support is provided through the message boards on the Association's website and also from the plethora of experience and information available by telephone, and the email access that we have to the Association's executive committee and secretariat.

They provide overall guidance to all members, rather than each school having to deal with issues on its own. I continue to be amazed at the number of members who do not make use of these basic facilities, and who do not regularly visit the Association's website: www.theisba.org.uk Wheels rarely need to be re-invented.

There are, however, issues that arise when the Association takes a lead on behalf of the members and, on occasions, for the wider independent sector under the ISC umbrella. These are generally issues of statutory and regulatory reform: for example, the introduction of a structured public benefit test for schools. They can also take the form of a response to decisions made by the courts, or other similar body: for instance the response to the Office of Fair Trading's enquiry into school fees in 2006. Over the years, the credibility of the Association as a consultee, representing the views both of the membership and the wider independent sector, has been increasingly recognised, and the involvement of ISBA is now frequently sought at an early stage.

As well as the general advice available to members, the Association produces a number of specific pieces of advice to which all members have access. *The Bursar's Guide* is a loose-leaf book that offers guidance on a wide range of issues related to the management of schools.

The document is written in general, rather than specific, terms: it covers chapters on the duties and qualifications of bursars; hardy perennials in a bursar's life; head and bursar relationships; relevant publications, references, and organisations; financial management of schools; direct taxation; value added tax; investment policy; the contract for educational services; scholarships and bursaries; charitable status and governors/trustees; employment law; insurance; catering; copyright; health and safety and welfare at work; fire safety; the maintenance of school buildings and grounds; and premises hire. The chapters are written by professionals in the field and are reviewed and updated regularly.

In addition to *The Bursars Guide*, the Association produces regular bulletins for members – usually eight each year. These deal with the issues of the day and provide up-to-date information on the same topics covered in the *Guide*. In addition, there is reporting on the meetings of the Association's executive committee; professional development opportunities; and recent appointments. The *Bulletins*, which used to be mailed to members, are now available for downloading to members from the website.

ISBA has recently added the provision of a set of model policies and procedures for member schools, with a particular focus on those necessary to satisfy the ISI regulatory requirements. All the model documents and policies, together with *The Bursar's Guide* and bulletins, as well as various one-off pieces of advice on a number of relevant and related issues, have now been gathered together to form a reference library on the members' area of the ISBA website.

The final document produced by the Association and distributed to members free of charge is *The Bursar's Review*. Three issues of this magazine are produced each year, one of which comprises the annual report and conference programme. The magazine is a less formal publication, with articles of topical interest contributed by both bursars and those providing professional advice and services to members. Whereas the other information referred to is essential reading, this magazine is generally more light-hearted: it includes various anecdotes and comments. Thus it provides a different view on the role and life of a bursar and constitutes a complementary vehicle for communication.

As well as the documentation prepared for members, the Association supports its membership through a wide and varied programme of professional development initiatives. The main event of the year is the Association's annual conference, which takes place over a couple of days each May. It is the largest of the various independent school associations' annual conferences, with some 400 delegates together with their spouses and partners.

As well as plenary sessions from distinguished speakers from the worlds of education, business and management, there are workshops on topical issues led by specialists in the field. An over-subscribed trade exhibition, usually with 80 to 100 suppliers of goods and services, provides a mutually beneficial opportunity for networking with each other, and professional colleagues and supporters of ISBA.

In addition, the annual general meeting of the Association and its annual dinner are held during these two days. While the executive committee and secretariat continually monitor and seek ways to develop and improve the conference, the feedback from members continues to reinforce the model, and only minor changes occur from year to year.

However, things change significantly through evolution and, over a longer period of evaluation, it is hard to imagine that current conferences held in Harrogate, Torquay and Edinburgh are the natural successor to the annual events for bursars only – no spouses in the 1980s – held at the Cambridge colleges. Maintaining the quality of the speakers is a perennial challenge – as is managing the disappointment of trade exhibitors who are unsuccessful in securing a trade stand. This opportunity to meet up with old colleagues, and to make friendships with new entrants to the profession, should not be missed – and that's before taking into account the value of the presentations and workshops.

Although the annual conference is the main event of the year, of equal importance is the programme of subject-specific professional development days arranged throughout the autumn and spring terms, and put on at different venues throughout England, making such courses accessible to all.

In my time as a bursar, the area that has seen most change is that associated with human resource management. Regular updates on this area of a bursar's responsibility are essential, as the law changes frequently and impacts on *all* employees. Year-on-year, HR days feature prominently in the seminar programme. In addition, there are regular update days on all other aspects of a bursar's range of responsibilities.

I make every effort to attend at least one of these a year, and I encourage my colleagues to do likewise. When compared with the prices charged by a number of commercial operators, the value for money that these days offer is significant. Even after one takes into account travel costs, and absence from the office, these are a most cost-effective method of keeping abreast of developments.

In early March each year, the Association runs a two day induction course for new bursars. Over recent years, attendees have included newly-appointed bursars about to take up post; recently appointed bursars in the early days of their careers; assistant bursars; and even a newly-appointed Head.

I did not attend this course when I was first appointed more than 18 years ago, but have since been a speaker, and sent my assistants as delegates. It is a thorough, if somewhat scary, introduction to the job, but should be considered as desirable – if not essential – for all newly appointed bursars. As well as seminars arranged by ISBA, a number of professional bodies put on their own seminars and training opportunities, and these are often promoted through ISBA and developed to address a particular identified need.

The final area of professional development opportunities that has been put in place for members consists of strategic partnerships with the Chartered Management Institute and the University of London's Institute of Education. Whilst recognising that the provision of job-related professional development was best delivered by the Association, it was felt that opportunities for wider and more formal management training, including an MBA in educational management, should be made available to members; these two organisations are most supportive of the Association, and work with it in developing opportunities particularly targeted to the membership.

The opportunities for new and innovative professional development are always under consideration, including a joint venture with the other Associations in the provision of leadership training. The continued developments in the use of the technology available to deliver some training by distance learning are also regularly reviewed. While there are some sacrifices in the reduction of opportunities for face-to-face networking, the costs and efficiency potential are significant.

As well as the national services provided by the ISBA secretariat, under the direction of the elected executive committee, there are, in most areas, local, informal groups of bursars meeting on a regular – usually termly – basis. Schools take it in turns to host their local group, which may vary in size from no more than half-a-dozen to over 70; a representative from the secretariat or executive committee is usually in attendance, and issues of the day are discussed, with particular emphasis on how they may impact on schools in a given locality or of a given type.

As a bursar operating in comparative isolation, it seems to me that there are two significant benefits from the services outlined thus far. First, the amount of formal advice through them that is available is considerable, and in itself it is worth significantly more than the cost of the annual subscription. While such advice can never be school-specific, it is reassuring to know that it has been produced by experienced professionals in the field; briefed and monitored by the experienced staff of the secretariat and the elected members of the executive committee, and validated by appropriate professional advisers to the Association.

Secondly, they give the opportunity to share problems with colleagues who have already experienced similar difficulties. A glance at the website's message board will see the same issues recurring time and time again, and in 99% of cases there will be a posting that says: 'I'll send a copy of my school's policy', or 'Give me a ring and I'll tell you how we dealt with a similar problem'.

Bursars are generally very open and honest in sharing their experiences, because as well as sharing solutions, they'll also share the potential pitfalls. You'll also see postings that say 'Don't make the same mistake as I did', and 'Give me a call, because I got it wrong'. This is an invaluable resource that helps in the development of best practice, and can save considerable time in dealing with issues as they arise.

I made reference in my introductory paragraphs to the membership criteria of the ISBA and the fact that membership is by school, rather than the individual. However, it is usual for the governing body to appoint the bursar as their representative. While this arrangement generally works well, it can become something of an issue from time to time because it means that the Association is very limited in the services that it can provide for individual bursars. It is not a trade union, and bursars are therefore encouraged to consider their position in this regard and to explore other opportunities for professional protection.

However, there are a few specific issues with which the Association can assist the individual. First, the Association has a number of retired and serving bursars who are able to help serving colleagues by appraising them. Within the library of documentation provided by ISBA is guidance on an appraisal process for bursars.

This includes a suggestion that schools might like to include the services of an experienced bursar to assist in the process, or even to carry it out on the Head's or governors' behalf. The secretariat holds a list of those who have indicated a willingness to offer this service which, if used, generally leads to a better-informed process and outcomes for the bursar being appraised.

The other main area of help that the Association can make available to individual bursars is the opportunity, in cases of employment difficulties involving the bursar, for a free 30-minute consultation with a solicitor. The length of the consultation may be extended in exceptional circumstances, and the consultation is arranged with one of a number of solicitors who are supporters of the Association. They are located all around the country.

The introduction is arranged by the general secretary, after considering the individual circumstances on a case-by-case basis. It is not the same as, and should not be confused with, detailed union advice, but it can provide a useful guide as to how specific employment issues for bursars might be resolved.

Before concluding this chapter, and to paraphrase President John F Kennedy: 'And so my fellow bursars: ask not what your Association can do for you – ask what you can do for your Association.'

While the secretariat provides a most professional and experienced service to bursars and their schools, their work is overseen by an elected executive committee of bursars who give of their time and experience voluntarily, to ensure that the Association develops in a direction that is relevant to the demands of the membership.

While we know that being a bursar gets ever more demanding on our time, we should consider, when possible, whether we can put something back into the profession. And for me, standing for election and becoming a member of the executive committee, and ultimately being chairman, meant that I got the ultimate from the ISBA: an inscribed pen, and tenure of the chairman's gavel for a year. However, much more importantly, I got the opportunity to learn so much from so many colleagues that I have since been able to take back, first to the school that supported my chairmanship, and subsequently to my current post.

And finally, remember that it is the *school* that is the member. While a lot of the information generated by the Association, the secretariat, the executive committee, and colleagues may only seem to be relevant to the bursar's job description, depending on how job descriptions are formally defined in your school, there are other senior management colleagues who could benefit from some of the information available – including some who aspire to being bursars or Heads themselves. Consider making the information available not only to senior management colleagues, but also to other members of your team: accountant, estates manager, catering manager, *etc*. In my experience, their development can also benefit from so much of the information that is available.

The ISBA is an essential resource to the efficient and effective operation of our schools. I urge you to use it as often and as widely as you can, and to participate fully in all that it offers.

Conclusion and overview

Jonathan Cook

What should be the abiding impressions left on readers by a book of this type? Those who cast their minds back to the introduction may recall being prepared for significant areas of overlap between individual contributions. There is a value in that state of affairs: it gives expert contributors the freedom to develop their chapters as they wish; it highlights the extent to which so many aspects of the work of a bursar and his/her team interact; it demonstrates the most pressing pre-occupations of those bursars in today's complex world.

It is worth reflecting on some of these recurring themes. Unsurprisingly, the *variety and growth* of the bursar's work are oft-repeated themes. Less obviously stated, but continually implied, is the level of *responsibility*: for the safety and wellbeing of the constituencies that make up a school community; for its financial health; for many aspects of its efficient administration and day-to-day running. Not only those, but also the *skills* needed – including the paramount need to deal effectively (sometimes diplomatically, or consensually; at other times, firmly and assertively) with a wide spectrum of people holding a multiplicity of roles.

Almost all the writers have pointed to the way in which the bursarial functions have grown over years or decades in terms of time demands, complication and expense. There is a recurring theme in how one balances the requirement to conform to regulations with the need for common sense. The word 'reasonable' dominates so much of our thinking and the legal requirements on us in today's world are formidable.

However, this very reasonability implies, and demands, a degree of discretion, judgement and decision-making that some people find daunting in a society that the older ones among us, at least, tend to feel is over-fearful and over-litigious. We have to keep a sense of proportion, whilst avoiding any suggestion that we are treating the law or regulatory requirements in a cavalier fashion.

One final thought. We would perhaps be mistaken ever to assume that the demands placed on the modern bursar are unique; indeed, chapter 1 listed some of those faced by bursars in earlier times. Recent books in this series have ended with a more tongue-in-cheek description of the role they have described, and our afterword picks up on this theme. Many of the daily situations that challenge bursars would be familiar to our predecessors.

In the early 1990s David Goucher, then bursar of Bryanston, wrote six articles for HMC's magazine *Conference & Common Room*, published by John Catt Educational Ltd. In them he gave a tongue-in-cheek picture of a bursar's dealings with the various constituencies that constitute a school community. The articles had a common title: 'The Bursar's Wicked Way'. We are very grateful to him for permission to reproduce extracts from them here.

Notice two things in particular. David Goucher's generation, too, faced a level of regulation which their bursar-predecessors would have found perplexing (much of it stemming from the demands of the Children Act 1989). And above all, once you have enjoyed his descriptions of dealing with Heads, teaching staff, parents, pupils and fellow-bursars, notice the more serious advice about ISBA with which he concludes – and compare it with what Paul Motte wrote in chapter 17. In a rapidly moving world, some things *don't* change.

Afterword

Extracts from *The Bursar's Wicked Way...*

David Goucher

1. ...With his Headmaster

Even if only metaphorically, I suspect that many bursars still stick a couple of exercise books down their trousers when invited to the Headmaster's study. Forty years on, childhood memories and experiences persist stubbornly into middle age, causing grown men to quake at the 'Beak's' door, searching their hitherto untroubled conscience for sins of omission or commission. To have any hope of successfully working your Wicked Way with your Headmaster, any such adolescent anxieties must be ditched from Day One.

Begin by putting yourself in his position. It is much more likely, however well-masked, that the poor fellow will be twitching with trepidation at the prospect of seeing you. Firstly, in his previous incarnation as a teacher, the Head will have held the bursar in substantially greater awe than any feeling of intimidation that you experience... It is very likely that he will have been cowed and bullied, perhaps even terrified by several bursars on the way up; furthermore, those uncomfortable encounters will have been reinforced by innumerable horrifying anecdotes (always apocryphal) of Headmasters whose lives have been made an absolute misery by their bursars.

Secondly, he will himself be nervous about being found out; not only because he will almost certainly have done something knowing full well that his action would not have had the bursar's approval, but also because his wealth of inexpertise in such matters as ball-cock valves, three-phase electricity, employment legislation, discounted cash flow projections, statutory sick pay, indemnity insurance, partial exemption from VAT, liability and gross redemption yields on investments will, at some stage in your conversation, become humiliatingly apparent.

Thirdly, the Headmaster's already exposed nerve endings will be on the point of spasm in the expectation that you have a disaster to report. "By the way, Headmaster, the Press has been on again." You already have a major advantage in the one-upmanship game: surrender it at your peril.

The subject of Head and bursar relationships never fails to crop up at HMC gatherings and bursars' conferences. Some bursars are convinced that Headmasters undergo some masonic ritual at their annual conference and return to their school sworn upon pain of disembowelment to put the bursar firmly in his place. In the worst case it is a master-slave relationship: in the best, more akin to a ship's captain and his first lieutenant.

But for those dedicated to the Art of Coarse Bursarship, the recommended analogy is that of patient and doctor. Ideally, the patient should be kept as still as possible; gently sedated; cheerfully reassured and beguiled increasingly into a state of total dependency. It should not be difficult to visualise the Head as someone in need of your tender ministry. Criticised by governors, pestered by parents and daily harassed by teachers, it is hardly surprising that many Headmasters relish the prospect of early retirement. Your ability and capacity to provide an antidote to so much suffering will be the measure of your success…

The occasion for really tweaking your antennae to maximum sensitivity is when the Head visits you in your office. You can be pretty sure that a battle has already been fought and lost, and your only role is that of damage limitation. You just have to pick up the pieces and avoid any indication of being judgemental. Plump up your patient's pillow; refresh his orange juice and compliment him on how well he is looking. Only *in extremis* should you seek a second opinion from the chairman of governors when, even then, it would be wise to do with the patient's consent.

For your future visits to the Head's study, instead of slipping a copy of Horace down your trousers, you should have at hand a prescribed course of multi-purpose medication which includes an anti-depressant; immunisation against viral contagion from over-exposure to teachers, pupils and parents; iron tablets to stiffen the backbone, and an elixir guaranteed to restore a ruddy complexion and cheerful countenance before the next batch of prospective parents arrives. You will surely find this approach infinitely more successful than sticking pins into a wax effigy.

2. ...With the common room

Teachers are uniquely different. All those years of tough and varied personnel management experience in industry, commerce or in the steamy jungles of Borneo or Malaya availeth nought. Forget the lot. There are just two lessons the bursar needs to learn to have any chance of survival, let alone success: the realisation that teachers are vocationally unmanageable, and an unquestioning acceptance that they are invariably right...

Warmth, understanding, tolerance, good humour, resilience, generosity, enthusiasm: you may still remember all those splendid attributes so carefully worked into your CV. So what happened to Mr Nice Guy? How come that you are now the character in the black hat? Inescapably and indelibly labelled 'The Bursar', you have become devious, partial, niggardly, sententious, remote, suspicious and high-handed. Even the most generous helpings of charm, sensitivity, sympathy and magnanimity go unrequited...

Now is the time to turn to the Art of Coarse Bursaring.

Rule *Number One*: Remember that "No" is a four-letter word. Much more effective is "I quite see the problem. Give me a few minutes and I'll get back to you". This will buy a little time either to attempt a quick fix or find somebody else to blame. Better still, "Can we discuss it after lunch?" well knowing that it is his only free afternoon, and he is already committed to the weekly shopping trip.

Then there are the pseudo-technical ploys: "Yes, I'm pretty sure that we could do what you want but just let me check the Fire/Safety/Policy; Legal/Building/Health and Hazard regulations," – especially the latter, which are a frightful mystery to everyone. Or: "What a good idea! I will definitely make sure that we put that forward for consideration (promising nothing) in next year's budget."

Number Two: Avoid open-ended questions, however seemingly innocuous. "How are things going, Michael?" Michael will grab you by the throat and tediously relate a series of incipient disasters that can only be avoided either by a new computer system; refurbishing his classroom completely; or by equipping the First Eight with the very latest marque of advanced boat technology. Serves you right for asking.

Number Three: Make a point of being seen around the school at night and during the weekend. It is a popular notion in the common room that bursars operate only from nine to five, Monday to Friday, with frequent absences for golf and race meetings. And when you do make your nocturnal visit, make jolly sure that it has been noticed. Bang shut half a dozen windows (there will be plenty to choose from) and turn off as many lights as time will allow. Bursars are notorious for their paranoid obsession with security and trivial economies; word of your visit will quickly spread. One or two visits a term should suffice nicely.

Number Four: Keep a very low profile from week ten onwards each term. Avoid appearing in public at all, day or night. The common room is no place at this time for even the boldest bursar. The notice board begins to look like the retreat from Moscow; reports stack daily higher; panic- driven notes fly around with all the subtlety and unerring inaccuracy of a Scud missile; nerves previously on edge are half-way down the cliff face and even "Good morning" is a veiled threat. This is most definitely not the moment for announcing your latest bright idea (*eg* writing on both sides of a piece of paper) or for experimenting with a new (*ie* cheaper) brand of coffee.

Number Five: Never, never, ever explain or attempt to justify a decision. You are bound to be on a loser. Teachers are much cleverer than you when it comes to an argument; it is a skill they are obliged to practise several hundred times a day in the classroom...

Number Six: This one is especially for all retired colonels, commanders and squadron leaders. Do not, under any circumstances, issue orders, directives or instructions to the common room. If there is one sure way of setting on edge the academic molar, it is to try to tell a teacher what he or she should, or should not, do. The wise bursar will instead offer guidance; invite co-operation; seek consensus; modestly venture an opinion; and never criticize. Remember: they are all performers, and they cannot stand a bad review. Always be generous with your praise.

If you can keep your Head on your side for most of the time; if you are invariably co-operative, courteous, supportive, patient and immediately on hand to resolve each and every crisis, there might just be a Get Well card from the common room while you are recovering from your first nervous breakdown.

3. ...With parents

Parents are characterised by their hopelessly unrealistic expectations of their offspring, and by the impossible demands they make on Headteachers, staff *in loco parentis* and classroom teachers in general. Schools would be so much happier places, one might be led to believe, were the pupil population made up entirely of orphans. That is one view...

The bursar, the realist in this educational wonderland, of course sees a quite different picture. Not to put too fine a point on it, parents are pretty important, providing the school's essential raw material, and the wherewithal to fund the annual budget. Thus, whilst teachers may choose to blame all their pupils' problems – and problem pupils – upon a disciplinarily ambiguous home background of repressive fathers and indulgent mothers, the bursar's general approach to parents must be one of respect, courtesy, sycophancy and unashamedly grovelling obsequiousness. They must be treated invariably as VIPs: Very Important Parents.

This is not to say that all parents are themselves models of perfection. Since they comprise a fairly high proportion of the human race, they may from time to time evince such human frailties as forgetfulness, evasiveness, mendacity and premeditated naiveté.

One hopeful father asked me, on the very first day of his son's entry into the school, how he might obtain a fee reduction on the grounds of financial hardship. Almost choking on a tuna sandwich, I politely offered him another chocolate bun and a second cup of tea, before patiently explaining that it is the over-ridingly essential function of parents (perhaps their *only* worthwhile function) to pay the school fees in full, not later than the first day of term. Moreover, I went on, the bursar's chief duty is to maximise income and minimise expenditure. Several cream cakes later, I had a new recruit to the school's Fees In Advance scheme.

Bursars undoubtedly need to be alive to the ingenuity, subterfuge and feral cunning frequently employed by some parents to obtain either grant assistance or fee remissions. I also have the impression that many parents, however well-heeled, have come to regard the payment of school fees in the same category as buying a new car, utterly convinced that no one ever pays the full list price. Others, having perjured themselves into gaining a place at an expensive school of their choice, then take the view that it is the school's obligation, and a requirement of its charitable status, to see a pupil through to univeristy, irrespective of either their means or willingness to meet the costs.

Your hesitant suggestion to impoverished parents that one of the many excellent (free) state schools might just be a viable alternative to the immediate penury they claim to be facing is received with total incredulity: "We could not possibly consider educating Simon or Amanda anywhere but here..." Beware also of promises to pay up in full in a couple of months' time; a leaking roof cannot be plugged with good intentions...

In reality, most are model parents who confidently, unquestioningly and quite amazingly hand over to the school their precious children and huge sums of money and who then return to Gerrards Cross or wherever, never to trouble us even once during the five years or so that follow. Yes, our parents are very special people. But should you still not be convinced, just consider what a nightmare it would be – as much for the Head as for the bursar – to work at a school which only admitted the children of school teachers. Think about it.

4. ...With pupils

Mercifully, the bursar is usually spared any immediate or direct regular contact with pupils... On the other hand, when pupils occasionally come to bursarial attention they do so in spectacular style, perhaps setting fire to the gymnasium in the middle of Speech Day or initiating food riots in the dining hall during the Prep School Headmasters' Open Day.

It would be quite unfair, however, and neurotically morbid, to view all pupils as embryonic arsonists or Red Faction terrorists. If not exactly models of impeccable conduct (except in the eyes of their parents), the majority of pupils work hard at keeping their heads well below the parapet, to avoid ever coming to the notice of 'authority'. Anyway, they have much more pressing preoccupations, such as what to wear at the Saturday night disco...

It is not uncommon for bursars to believe that, in their absence, the school cannot possibly function for more than a few hours without crumbling apart. Moreover, being next to God in the staff hierarchy, it is uncomfortably deflating to learn that none of the pupils even knows your name, let alone has any idea about what you actually *do*. For the most part, they see the bursar as a remote, grey-haired, grey-suited representative of officialdom, with a peculiar habit of standing up straight and dressing conservatively: something of a Dickensian dodderer who merges imperceptibly into the fabric of the school's oldest buildings.

Keep it that way. This is an invaluable perception and fundamental to your strategy. You may already have lived to regret your open door policy with the common room and bursarial staff; the last thing you should now want is to allow the opportunity for 700 or so assorted adolescents to poke your shirt front with their puerile demands...

Above all, remember that it is neither your job nor should it be your wish, however sorely tempted, to correct pupil misbehaviour. Should you happen upon some blatant abuse of school rules which cannot be ignored, perhaps a loosely-knotted tie, hands in pockets or a shirt not tucked in, a disdainfully raised eyebrow should suffice. It might be worth practising this in front of a mirror to avoid any possibility of sending out a confusing message. The bursar is inescapably regarded by pupils as a person of authority: try not to disillusion them. Growing up is a painful enough process without your adding uncertainty to their cherished perceptions.

Just when you thought that you had won your wicked way with the student body and turned your attention to the more important business of reducing your golf handicap, in come the social engineers with their Charter of Children's Rights. Children's 'rights' for goodness sake! As one brought up on the King James version, I had always believed that by definition children had no rights. Children did as they were told, without question, and were well advised to keep their complaints and opinions to themselves.

Alas, no longer. Now, unless they have a choice of wholemeal bread and skimmed milk at every meal, or if the bath water occasionally runs cold, the little blighters are ringing up *Childline*... Having endured the first round of

DSS inspections, it is now clear that the demands of The Children Act in terms of pupil privacy, space, comfort, ambience, hygiene, health and safety are so formidable that, were the same criteria applied to the children's parental homes, most would be closed down tomorrow.

Even picking up litter may be outlawed as a punishment unless the pupils are issued with protective clothing and first undertake appropriate safety training and certification. The bursar, not being protected by The Children Act, may of course continue to stuff his pockets with the detritus ignored by studiously unobservant teachers.

Children are also, by nature, revolutionaries and anarchists who need to be pacified by frequent doses of bursarial bromide. By being generous with the calories, tweaking up the temperature settings and keeping windows closed as an energy conservation policy, it should be possible to induce a state of near total torpidity amongst the student body.

5. ...With other bursars

A visiting speaker at a recent ISBA annual conference flatteringly likened bursars to swans: elegant and serene on the surface, but paddling furiously underneath. This was perceptive, as well as flattering. While few would admit to it, bursars are certainly conscious of their image. This is not normally a matter of personal vanity, albeit that many will have a tube of Grecian 2000 and a range of expensive aftershave unguents in their bathroom cabinet: it is much more a concern for the reputation of their school and an indication of striving to attain the expectations that others have of 'The Bursar'.

The governors look for someone who is financially skilled and experienced: preferably with an architectural and engineering background; a successful track record in business, personnel management, law, or industrial relations and – while medical qualifications are not normally required – preferably someone who is pretty good at extracting blood from stones. Above all, the governors want someone who is sound...

Most Headmasters, it would seem, want a compliant seven-days-a-week workhorse who can deal with all those dull and burdensome non-academic chores – catering, domestic services, health and safety, insurance, security and estate maintenance – with the briefest hint of direction but without anything being done that might remotely upset or offend a member of the common room. And when the going gets a little rough, the bursar's shoulder needs to be there to cry on.

The common room want someone rather like the Archangel Gabriel: miracle worker; infinitely understanding, tolerant and forgiving; ubiquitous and omnipresent; generously indulgent of their minor failings (having, for example, run the House pocket money account into the red, three terms in succession), and even more generous with the supply of photocopiers, video machines, computers, telephones, coffee, travelling expenses, responsibility allowances and innumerable other benefits-in-kind. Teachers want a bursar who, though friendly, never becomes too matey since, when things do not go quite to plan, who better to blame for their own shortcomings?

Chums and equal fellow-sufferers we may be, but there are inevitably those who wish to demonstrate that they are more equal than others. Appropriate put-down ploys should therefore be developed for use in the appropriate circumstances. Here are a few examples.

Chummy: we begin with those bursars who are inclined to wear their illustrious school name as a formal title. You might have telephoned a colleague, and a somewhat haughty voice comes to the line: "Lanchester here." This form of introduction, more normally associated with bishops and peers of the realm, can be quite daunting. You must immediately grab the initiative. Begin by asking if you are speaking to the bursar. Of course you are. "Hi, Mike, how are things?" "Sorry, you seem to have the wrong name," comes the aggrieved reply. Of course you do. "Anthony James here."

Great. You now have him uneasily on first name terms. Before putting down the telephone, remember to ask his name again – thus undermining his conviction that he is known and revered throughout the world of independent education. Also, without appearing to be the school dunce, you might enquire exactly where Lanchester is located, in case you might wish to drop by when you are next in the vicinity.

Hot Air: we all know the bursar who, quite unintentionally I am sure, can be a bit of a know-all. Let us call him Alex Smarthouse. He turns up at group and regional meetings with sheaves of paper, pamphlets galore and a whole library of technical tomes. He will have proposed at least six topics for discussion, each one tabled to demonstrate his mastery of the latest legislation on, say, VAT exemptions, the Financial Services Act, new employment law or whatever. The more he drones on, the more you might become convinced of your own professional inadequacy.

Do not allow yourself to become disheartened. Having allowed him to enjoy a smug smile of satisfaction, this is the moment for mentioning that you have heard, from some very vague source, that the Health and Safety Executive (or was it the European Parliament?) has recently regulated a new type of air passage valve for hot water boilers, to prevent a possible cause of Legionnaire's Disease. Moreover, it has been rumoured that schools might face closure if the new valves have not been fitted within six months. You say that you would welcome advice from anyone who might have more detail. Like yourself, nobody will have the faintest idea what you are talking about.

Alex, however, will have been making frantic notes and will probably be perspiring visibly at this point. Now *you* are the one with the satisfied smile; confident that the poor chap will spend hours, possibly days, poring over Croner's Manuals, telephoning the local authority offices and delving into hundreds of HSE guidance booklets in search of the holy grail.

Job's comforter: do you find it as surprising as I do to discover just how many bursars seem so keen to acquaint colleagues with their personal tribulations? They bang on remorselessly about their inordinately long working hours; the number of years since they last took a holiday, or the latest example of ineptitude and lunacy emanating from their school's common room. What do they hope to gain from such masochistic moaning? Sympathy? Awe? Admiration? Are they seeking to impress by demonstrating a huge capacity for work, or to win your pity for their self-denying dedication?

The true exponent of the Art of Coarse Bursarship must have no truck with point-scoring of this sort. Do not, for example, retaliate by relating the circumstances of the governors' meeting which ran for a whole weekend, nor the story of the teacher who blamed the bursar for his not having been registered to vote in the General Election (can they do nothing for themselves?).

Far better to let them stew in their suffering, perhaps adding to their self-mortification by mentioning that you have just returned from a three week holiday in Nepal (during term-time, of course) and how very much you are looking forward to next week's trade invitations to Henley, Lord's and Wimbledon: "Will you be there? I suppose not." Nothing is to be gained by your implying either inadequacy or inefficiency on their part: passing mention of a good book dealing with management by delegation might not, however, come amiss.

Self-evident it may be, but there is little hope of achieving your wicked ways with the Bursarial Brotherhood unless you make a point of being seen at the annual ISBA conference and all the local, regional and national bursars' meetings. Even if you cannot make it for the seminars, or to soak up the wisdom of the visiting speakers, make jolly sure that you turn up for the golf match, all of the drinks parties and the black tie dinners.

After all, the really worthwhile benefit on these occasions comes not from the platform but from picking the brains of fellow bursars who have diligently sought out the best buys or who have produced the perfect policy document on school security or risk assessment.

Unlike most professions, it is astounding how generous bursars are in helping each other and sharing the benefit of their hard-won expertise and experience. Never be too shy nor too proud to seek help or advice from colleagues: not only can they contribute handsomely to your primary objective of a care-free and comfortable life but, flattered by being asked to advise, you will have extended your circle of friends and the choice of overnight hospitality *en route* to your next day out at the races. That reminds me: I must give Tony a ring at Lanchester.

If there is any furious paddling to be done, do delegate it to someone else. In this way, not only will you appear serene and unruffled above the water line, you will have achieved that state of bursarial grace whereby you may swan smoothly through the day and glide effortlessly towards your pension.

6. ...With governors

We intend to use David Goucher's sixth piece as the afterword to the next book in this series – which happens to be on governors and governance.

Heads **£12.50**
Edited by Brenda Despontin
and Nigel Richardson
ISBN: 978 1 904724 49 0

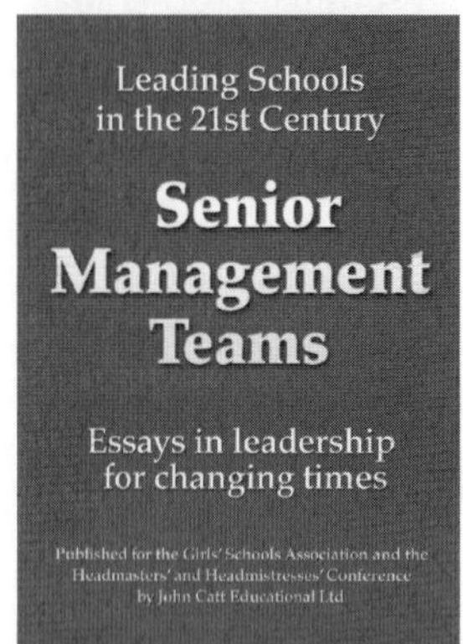

Senior Management Teams **£12.50**
Edited by Brenda Despontin
and Nigel Richardson
ISBN: 978 1 904724 59 9

Leading Schools
in the 21st Century
Heads of
Department
Essays in leadership
for changing times
Published for the Girls' Schools Association and the
Headmasters' and Headmistresses' Conference
by John Catt Educational Ltd

Heads of Department **£12.50**
Edited by Brenda Despontin
and Nigel Richardson
ISBN: 978 1 904724 65 0

Newly Qualified Teachers **£12.50**

Edited by Judith Fenn
and Nigel Richardson
ISBN: 978 1 904724 735

Pastoral Work **£12.50**

Edited by Hilary Moriarty
and Nigel Richardson
ISBN: 978 1 904724 803

Public Relations, **£12.50**
Marketing and Development

Edited by Nigel Richardson
with Tory Gillingham and Nick Pettingale
ISBN: 978 1 904724 94 0

NOTES